✸ *Naked Soul*

Uncovering the Mystery of the Soul

Mark C. Tolbert

Victorious Living
Publishing Co.

Copyright © 2002 by Mark C. Tolbert.
All rights reserved.
Printed in the United States of America.
No part of this book may be used or reproduced in any manner whatsoever without written permission except in the case of brief quotations embodied in the text reviews. For information address Victorious Living Publishing Company, 3400 Paseo Boulevard, Kansas City, Missouri 64109.

Library of Congress Cataloging-in-Publication Data
Tolbert, Mark C.
Naked Soul: Uncovering the Mystery of the Soul/Mark C. Tolbert—1st ed.
Includes Index, Endnotes, bibliographical references
ISBN 0-9716694-0-6
1. Religious.   2. Spiritual Growth—Inspirational

DEDICATION

To Marky, my namesake.

As he was developing into manhood, I was growing into fatherhood. Often, it seemed more like "practicing" than a honed skill. Thank you for your patience and understanding.

Just as we were ready to bond at another level, you left to live in Paradise.

Marky, we miss you and will never forget you. Your "homegoing" gave me a fresh sense of eternity.

I know you are choosing your fine family mansion. Your mother taught you well.

I love you, Marky, and will see you soon.

Acknowledgments

My wife of 23 years, Emelda, has shown her loving support, prayers, and patience. My son, Britton, has "put up with me" as I have missed some of his sporting events. Both have shown understanding when I spent countless hours talking with everyone I could about the soul. They endured late nights while I researched and wrote.

I want to thank so many people for their encouragement, prayers, and constant support. Pastor Tommy Barnett inspired my first writing of a "soul winning" manual. This gave me courage to follow my search for the revelation of the soul. My mother, Lorene Tolbert, and father, Bishop Lee A. Tolbert, inspired me to conquer my fears and remove obstacles. My good friends, Bishop Charles Ellis III, Bishop Clifford Frazier, and Bishop Noel Jones have stood by me for many years.

As I continue to grow spiritually, my siblings continue to show loving support and understanding. From oldest to youngest, they are Lee, Jr., Wendell, Vivian, Carol, and Aaron. Vivian and her husband John Roper gave me the blessed opportunity to travel to Clinton, Iowa. I received God's significant revelation about the soul en route.

The Christ Temple Church family members—too numerous to name—continue to stay by my side. Thank you for your prayers, unfailing support, and love.

Special thanks to Dr. Martis Jones and Le´Rhonda Collier who have been tireless workers to help me bring this comprehensive project to full fruition.

Selah.

Foreword

What a tremendous opportunity I have been afforded. God has given me the gift of knowledge about such a subject as the soul. It affects every human being that has ever walked the face of the earth.

Adam and Eve were the first living souls created by God. They tried to clothe their nakedness after their fall from grace. Although this book does not deal in detail with that dimension of the soul, we must know that every soul is naked before Almighty God. No matter what we wear or how we try to hide, this is true.

This book will answer a lot of questions that people have asked in general about the soul, especially when a loved one dies. It is then that their curiosity yearns to have some assurance that what they have heard for years is really true: The soul goes back to eternity to be with God.

This exposé is intended to put to rest your questions, your doubts, and even your fears about the present and future of the soul. Every male and female is born with an eternal soul, and it is for us to know the mystery about it.

As I researched and asked questions about the soul for over seven years, I thought I had taken on an impossible mission. Many people had thoughts and wonderful ideas about the soul. None had the full answer. One day God asked me, "Would you like to know where your soul is?"

Early in the book you will read about my conversations with God. In the last chapter you will learn about an earlier prophecy that spurred me on to finish what God had started when He led me to write this eyeopener about the soul.

After the tragic death of my older son Mark C. Tolbert, Jr. ("Marky"), I fully understood what Prophet Mitchell had prophesied. Without knowing about Prophet Mitchell, Dr. Martis Jones said, "Well, I guess you have one more chapter to write."

Immediately, I recalled the prophecy of Prophet Mitchell. I knew I had to write the last chapter on two men's souls. This compelling chapter describes the special bond between Marky and me, and how the revelation about eternity and his soul transformed my life.

I pray that you will be blessed as you discover the deep knowledge about the soul revealed in this book.

✶ Contents

INTRODUCTION   1

CHAPTERS

1. Truth or Consequences   7
2. The Flesh   11
3. A Roundabout Revelation   19
4. The Scene and Unseen   27
5. Enter Ye   35
6. The War Is On   45
7. Languages of the Soul—Part One   57
8. Languages of the Soul—Part Two   63
9. Languages of the Soul—Part Three   69
10. Receiving God's *IS_{NESS}*   77
11. Your Satisfied Soul   83
12. Caring for the Soul   89
13. The Souls of Two Men   95

CHAPTER NOTES   105

INDEX   107

ABOUT THE AUTHOR   111

✳ *Naked Soul*

Uncovering the Mystery of the Soul

Mark C. Tolbert

Victorious Living
Publishing Co.

✵ Introduction

You are fearfully and wonderfully made, and your soul knows it.

As God admired His new creation, He exclaimed with delight, "It is good!" It was good and very good because this perfect creation—man—was made in the image and after the likeness of God—good.

God shaped His handiwork from particles of dust. The dust was from the earth and it was reddish in color. The transliteration of the Hebrew word for red earth or ground is *Adamah*. God piled up *Adamah* and shaped it in the form of a man. At that point the man was only a form and had reality only to God. This man had no life, no breath, and no mobility. It was only a still, lifeless form. However still or lifeless, this form was valuable to God because it was destined to be created in His own image—good and perfect.

As He completed His handiwork, God breathed His Spirit into the dust nostrils of the man form. Instantaneously it became charged with life, and life became a reality to the previously inanimate form (Genesis 2:7). It became a breathing, living reality to God. And what a life it was. God named this marvelous mobilized man of life **Adam** (from *Adamah*).

God did not stop with His creation of Adam. He continued to create an ideal environment replete with enchantment, beauty, comfort, and charm. He planted and grew a lush verdant garden. He strategically placed and set in motion gently flowing rivers for drink and watering. And He formed precious gold metals and stones.

God had richly rendered all the abundant accouterments for Adam, yet felt He still had not completed this ideal environment for His magnificent handiwork. He wanted to provide more deeply for Adam on the personal level. As He looked upon Adam, He said, "It is not good that man should be alone. I will make an help meet for him" (Genesis 2:18). God made woman from Adam's rib. She, too, was filled with the life and Spirit of God. He brought her to Adam, and Adam passionately and proudly pronounced, "This is now bone of my bones, and flesh of my flesh: she shall be called Woman, because she was taken out of Man" (Genesis 2:23). This first woman became the mother of all living.

A New Beginning

Adam and his newly created companion Eve lived, loved, and enjoyed the fullness and abundance of their absolutely perfect environment. They walked naked through their paradise and were found innocent before each other, and before God. They knew no evil. They were free from sin. They knew no guilt. Humankind and the surroundings were pure and sanctioned by the presence of the perfect God. The whole—soul, spirit, and human flesh—interrelated in complete harmony. What a wonderful state of being.

Everything was perfect. Everyone was happy. Everything was fine. Or was it? Let's take another look.

First, Eve represented the love of God in action. She was created to complement, augment, and balance the male characteristics of the Adam man. Being a refinement of man, this woman represented the feeling nature—sentiment, sensitivity, and tenderness—the mother principle of God in expression.

Neither Eve nor Adam was an arbitrary or capricious act of God. Instead, when He consciously created them, God had a definite purpose and plan to fulfill. He created them as individuals in union—perfect, complete, and whole. Morally upright creations, their primary purpose for existence was to reflect the glory of God.

Second, Adam and Eve were to oversee the rest of God's creations. These included the fish of the sea, the fowl of the air, the cattle and beast, and everything else that crept on the earth (Genesis 1:24-26). In essence, Adam and Eve were privileged to partake of a perfect place, Paradise—The Garden of Eden. Through their God-likeness, they were given dominion over the plant and animal kingdoms in their interactions with nature. God instructed them on what to eat and how to live: perfect, holy, and morally upright.

As with any job description, binding agreement, contract or covenant, we are given a responsibility and some accountability to abide by the terms given. Adam and Eve's job description was to be fruitful, multiply, and replenish the earth. God told them clearly and specifically not to eat of the tree of the knowledge of good and evil. God distinctly stated that to eat of the fruit of that particular tree would bring a sure consequence—death. That is, an immediate spiritual death and a physical death over time.

However, if God made His handiwork perfect and put them in a perfect place for living and loving, how could anything go wrong? Let's step back once again to Genesis 2:7.

> *And the Lord God formed man of the dust of the ground, and breathed into his nostrils the breath of life; and man became a living soul.*

Take a moment and think on these words, "God breathed into his nostrils the breath of life. When God breathed His breath into man's nostrils, he became a living soul." Now, close your eyes and think about this more deeply. Ask God to reveal to you what this meant then and what it means to you now.

This was the beginning of the human *soul*.

The breath of God was His Spirit that gave "life." This Life given by God's Spirit made man a living reality to God and to himself. Before then, man was merely a formation of red earth (*Adamah*). He was God's creation, yet was immobile and inactive. Just formation. God's Spirit-breath gave life. Life gave vitality to body cells, tissues, organs, blood, a pumping heart, and a brain containing the mind. Teeth, tendons, and muscles began to form and function with perfection. All form became materialized, mobilized, and realized from the power of the breath of God. Thereby, Adam received life from God, and not of himself. From this Spirit-breath of God emerged a living soul.

What About Your Soul?

Think about it. God's spirit brought God-life to Adam, and he became a living soul. The human soul, also referred to as the human psyche, contains personality, emotions, and individuality. The soul—not the flesh—is a person's reality and the beginning of a person's preparation for eternity. Because the soul is eternal, we must come to the enlightenment that the real person (*self* or "me") is locked inside the earthly shell. The creation of the soul was also the beginning of decision-making and choice-making for humankind. This is sometimes referred to as "free will," or the God-given ability to choose. Choice was part of God's plan for Adam and Eve.

However, the morally upright station of man and woman crumbled when Adam and Eve exercised a "less than good" choice for the soul. One day, while living peacefully in the Garden of Eden, Eve, Adam's *helpmate,* was approached by a colorful captivating serpent. As it got closer to Eve, it asked her whether God had *really* told her and Adam not to eat of every tree in the garden. When Eve told the serpent that she and Adam were strictly forbidden to eat of the tree for fear of punishment by death, he slyly slipped in, "Ye shall not surely die" (Genesis 3:4). He continued his lie-stretching by telling Eve that their knowledge would actually increase in equality with God's knowledge (Genesis 3:1–7). Keep in mind that Adam had spoken to God and heard God through his natural ears, but had never seen the God behind the voice.

Eve's choice—a primal human exercise in decision-making—was to begin to doubt, question her dominion over animals, and to reason. She turned her attention away from the awareness of her God-likeness and opened herself to the serpent's great cunning. She yielded, and being Adam's helpmate, advised Adam to yield. Their capricious act was unwise, and certainly not Spirit-led. Their disobedience was the fall of man and woman from their morally upright state. Their bad choice separated them from the good with which God had so resplendently surrounded and entrusted to them.

However, before they made their bad choice, Adam and Eve had been following the Spirit of God—absolute good. They did not see or succumb to the impressions of the outer world. Their souls completely harmonized with and followed only the Spirit of God, and they kept their original created state—perfect and morally upright.

As soon as Adam and Eve broke the covenant, they began to see duality—both good and evil and life and death. They began an immediate spiritual decline, seeing evil in a similar manner as loomed by their evil decision. They lost their innocence. They felt the pang of guilt and the emotion of embarrassment from their senseless decision. They began to deteriorate by a slow physical death.

Responsible for their disobedience, Eve and Adam were lost to themselves, individually and collectively. They were lost to God. They no longer knew themselves as they had before—good, innocent, and pure. Seeking to hide from God, they fled the pristine environment they had once enjoyed and ended up in an unknown land far from their original surroundings. They experienced evildoing, pain, and ugliness. They were left to clothe themselves, look out for their livelihood, and fend for themselves. What a far cry from paradise, peace, joy, and radiant life.

Adam and Eve transformed from "good and very good" to not so good. Their original sin left an indelible mark on the human soul. However, today our souls do not have to be destined for destruction and eternal damnation. This book will show you *why* and *how*.

1

✵ Truth or Consequences

For the first time, the parents of the entire human race, Adam and Eve, thrust themselves into suffering. This created a tenacious tapestry interlaced with perfection and imperfection. It was intricately woven with travesty, dilemma, and destruction, with phases showing: 1) *souls in paradise;* 2) *perfection in everything;* 3) *safety at home;* 4) *protection and provision;* 5) *no awareness of temptation;* 6) *temptation overtakes the spirit;* 7) *yielding and disobedience to God;* 8) *immediate spiritual death;* 9) *feeling lost;* and 10) *slow death over time.*

Adam and Eve's consequence was passed down to their remote offspring, the whole human race. The human soul runs a course similar to that of Adam and Eve while discerning whether to follow things that are temporal or eternal. In the Garden, the crafty serpent's temptation was temporal. But Adam and Eve failed to pay heed to that which was eternal—the tree of life. They yielded to the temporal—"the tree of knowledge of good and evil" (Genesis 2:9). This brought an immediate spiritual death and a long physical death over time.

Often when we are tempted by the devil, it is when things are going well. The temptation causes us to doubt and to consider something seemingly better. The key question to answer is, "Is this really better or only an appearance of some good?"

Many biblical characters faced soulful struggles between temporal and eternal. Esau sold his birthright (eternal) for a piece of meat (temporal). Out of jealousy, Joseph's brothers sold him into slavery; Ahab and Jezebel chose idolatry over worshiping God; David had Uriah killed in battle so he could marry his wife Bathsheba; drunk with wine, King Ahasuerus dethroned his wife Queen Vashti for insubordination (she refused to whimsically show off her beauty); Samson relinquished his strength to sex and lust.

What About Our Souls?

Each of us has a soul, and it is eternal. Each soul goes through cycles similar to those of tried and tested biblical characters. Their stories are our true stories—the good, the bad, the sad, and the ugly. Our souls journey from paradise found to paradise lost and regained. We struggle with things temporal and eternal on our paths to find the sacredness within ourselves, our brothers and sisters in this family of life, and in our Creator. These depict our sacred soulful days. Yet we still struggle to know more about the soul. We anxiously ask ourselves and others: What is the soul? Where is the soul? What does my soul look like? How can I contact my soul?

These things that we cannot necessarily see about our souls are revealed to us through the eternal wisdom of God. With faith, we must seek God through prayer and Scripture to reveal every aspect of our souls. The Word of God reveals knowledge about the soul and how to tap its wisdom to communicate with the soul.

Scriptures show the eternal aspect of the soul. For example, the book of Lamentations is replete with words of comfort, peace, and assurance about the soul. In Lamentations 3:20, 24, 25, and 26, we find that the soul is nourished with hope, compassion, and the salvation of the Lord. As we continue to seek the vast array of Scriptures that show us our *soulfulness* and our soulful journey, we discover more about God, ourselves, the sacredness of others, and the language of the soul.

Because our soul is drawn toward these answers, we must search for and anticipate them. Each soul will not rest until it finds that which it longs for, and that is why in Lamentations we find that the Lord is good to those of us who wait for Him. He is good to the soul that seeks Him. As we seek Him through prayer, meditation, fasting, consecration, thanksgiving, praise, worship, and reading and rightly dividing the Word of God, we maintain the hope of God's promise that He rewards those who deftly and diligently seek Him (Hebrews 11:6).

Also, God said that He will continue to open the windows of heaven and pour out upon us—for the blessing of our souls—an abundance of anointing and rich rewards as we seek Him. We find an affirmation in Isaiah 26:8-9: ". . . O Lord, have we waited for thee; the desire of our soul is to thy name, and to the remembrance of thee. With my soul have I desired thee in the night; yea, with my spirit within me will I seek thee early."

The Psalmist's soul waited and groaned for God with, "My heart panteth . . ." (Psalm 38:10) and "As the hart panteth after the water brooks, so panteth my soul after thee, O God" (Psalm 42:1). The soul's true longing is for the eternal—not the temporal. It is fulfilled by an intimate relationship with God.

Let us not be vexed, agitated, or waxed with worry about the Fall as it regards Adam and Eve. Although we know they are the parents of the entire human race, and their consequences have been passed down to us, their remote offspring, we can be encouraged with the hope of the saving of our souls through God's love, mercy, and grace.

With the punishment of Adam and Eve God gave the promise of redemption. He said, "And I will put enmity between thee [the serpent] and the woman, and between thy seed and her seed; it shall bruise thy head, and thou shall bruise his heel" (Genesis 3:15). This points us to the promise of the birth of

Jesus that was to take away the sins of the world, and thus redeem humankind and remake us in a spiritual sense.

Through redemption, justification, the death, and resurrection of Jesus Christ, God replaced our sinful Adamic nature with His divine nature. By accepting Jesus Christ, we remove that which is displeasing to God and, in turn, renew the harmony between God and us (propitiation). This brings satisfaction in His sight, and we restore the intimate fellowship with Him. This is the kind of lasting satisfaction the soul longs for and seeks.

In every soul Christ is the hope of glory . . .

—(from Colossians 1:27 NIV)

2

✸ The Flesh

Let's briefly return to the Garden. When the sly serpent asked Eve whether God had *really* told her and Adam they should not eat of every tree in the garden, she had a choice. Eve could have answered or ignored the serpent. She chose to answer. At that point she turned her attention away from her spirit of divine wisdom. The serpent won her attention. Being subtle and "slick," he caused her to doubt God's words. He convinced her to believe she and Adam "would not surely die." He then insinuated himself into her confidence and deceived her by stating that their knowledge would actually "increase in equality with God's knowledge."

Think about it: The all-knowing, everywhere-present, and all-powerful God safeguarded and secured Adam and Eve's dominion and authority over the animals of Eden. Yet Eve chose to enter into discourse, debate, and persuasion with one of her subjects. This one—the serpent—was subtler than any of the beasts of the field. When God made Adam and Eve, he finished a perfect handiwork of wholeness in body, soul, and spirit. The body was to be subject to soul and spirit. The serpent was to be subject to Adam and Eve—not the serpent asking about or advising or addressing Eve or Adam on their livelihood or lifestyle. God did not intend for them to be chummy or to interact as equals with those He had placed them over—all living creatures.

Humankind Must Take Notice

The serpent represents seduction and sensation. It evokes the senses through its vibrant colors, hissing sound, "slickness," and sensuous movement. Its subtle nature caught Eve off guard, gained entry into her consciousness and swept through her soul, convincing her to do what she knew was wrong.

Eve represents the soul that is attracted to sensation and promises of pleasure. When this attraction developed into a trap (disobedience, distorted thinking, deceit, and sin), Eve became ensnared with the delusory proposition of the serpent rather than God's safe and secure promises of paradise and bliss. Her focus shifted from the words of truth that God had given to her and Adam to a lie. This caused her to lose sight of her authority, power, and dominion over the outer and the inner—Eden and her own soul.

When we fail to follow God's way, we too weaken our mastery over outer sensations and attractions. And we surely suffer the consequences. Just as with Adam and Eve, when we deviate from God's commandments, we put ourselves in an emotional and physical prison of pain, *dis-ease,* and spiritual death. The choices that we make about our body of flesh could make us miss out on this eternal promise of life in heaven and eternal life with Jesus Christ. For it is the flesh that gets mad. It is the flesh that doubts. It is the flesh that says if it feels good, do it. The flesh lures us away from the things of God and gets us caught up in the damnable dictates, doctrines, and traditions of misguided persons and evildoers. Their ways are lifeless and not of Spirit. Followed too tenaciously or for too long they can cause spiritual and physical death.

Why does it seem like our flesh has more power than our spirit? From all of my pastoral work and counseling church members, I have found it is because we take more time to pamper, primp, powder, and feed the flesh than we do the human spirit. We pay more attention to prompts of unruly flesh than we do the promises of Holy Spirit. When we think about feeding the flesh, we think about burgers and fries, steak and eggs, lobster and shrimp, or whatever our taste may call for. If we are not feeding it with food, we respond to the flesh directly through our feeling nature.

In fact, the flesh is the entity that lures us to have appetites for pornography, adulterous affairs, and fornication. As we feed and fuel the flesh, we keep ourselves in a spiritual warfare, and not flesh and blood warfare. Though I am a strong proponent of healthy eating, good nutrition, and a balanced diet, my stronger position is rooted and grounded in feeding the soul. Feasting on the God-directed menu (Word of God), given for our spirit and soul, matters much more than filling up on chicken tenders, strip steaks, or hot dogs for the outer human body.

The verses in 1 John 2:23–25 show us it is so important to abide in the ways of the Spirit of God, and not humans. We must "continue in the Son and in the Father" while staying consistent in our belief in the power of the Spirit, because "this is the promise that he hath promised us, *even* eternal life."

It is so vital to our eternal existence that we begin to follow the diet for our spirit and soul development and unfoldment. As he wrote about the problems of the flesh in Romans 7:18, Paul said, "For I know that in me dwelleth no good thing: for to will is present with me; but how to perform that which is good I find not." He continued with, the spirit is willing, but the flesh is weak. Paul also said that he was carnal—"sold under sin."

The things that Paul knew were right to do, and thus intended to do, were the very things he did not do, yet knew to do them. However, we must not give an excuse, "If Paul, an Apostle, could not command his flesh to subjection, how much harder is it for us to do so?" I say, eschew such alibis. You are not Paul, and neither am I. The commandments of God are still spiritual and we must obey them. God is for us, and no flesh can win against us.

Just as our body needs vitamins, minerals, amino acids, and various trace elements to be strong and healthy, so does our spirit need nourishment. Our spirit person will be overtaken by flesh until we put our foot down and demand that the flesh get under subjection to the nourishment of the Holy Spirit. We must equip our spirit to receive the guiding of Spirit, and then follow through likewise.

It is essential that you grasp this because the body is here on earth for a short time, and when we die, it goes back to the substance from which it was formed—dust of the ground. The body is temporary. The soul's home is eternal, and as "It is the Spirit that quickeneth; the flesh profiteth nothing" (John 6:63). The Holy Spirit gives eternal life. The human soul lives on forever.

Let's Do Battle

". . . The weapons of our warfare are not carnal, but mighty through God to the pulling down of strong holds" (2 Corinthians 10:4). When we get ready to launch an all-out attack on the power of the flesh, we are not going to take a gun and blow off our own heads in order to win the battle. We are not going to call the police and have ourselves arrested. As we work to conquer and overcome the fleshly battles, we must constantly tell the flesh the weapons of our warfare are not carnal. They are spiritual, and when we reach for the anointing oil, we give the flesh a surprise attack. The flesh doesn't get upset because it does not realize that we are bringing it into subjection to the Holy Spirit.

The same is true when the flesh craves unhealthy food. What flesh does not know is that we have pushed back our plate, tamed our cravings, and put it under subjection to our spirit of obedience to Christ. We have ordered flesh and all its attributes to be commanded by the Spirit of Christ that lives in us so that we may be conquerors. This is when we tap our greatest potential—the Spirit of Christ working in and through us for victory over the flesh.

As for me, I refuse to use the weapons that tip off the flesh as to what is coming, but I will subdue the flesh like Delilah subdued Samson. I will not struggle. I will simply push back my plate, fast, and pray until the transformation takes place in my life. Then, when I say "greater is He that is in me than He that is in the world," it will be because I have gained the victory over my flesh through the spirit man as it is led, guided, and fed by the Holy Spirit.

No one will ever need to engage in a street fight, a cursing out, or turning over or throwing a piece of furniture when he or she learns how to subdue the flesh (our greatest enemy) through spiritual warfare.

I will always remember when my older son Marky (Mark, Jr.) was a little boy and went to the grocery store (we did not call them supermarkets at that time) with my father (Grandpa). While they shopped and filled the grocery cart, Grandpa was in his usual character (showing his kindness and good spirit seen only after I got grown and out of the house). As grocery selections continued, Marky took the lead—both in pushing the cart and placing in food items.

When they arrived home, Mother began digging to the bottoms of the many sacks. She was looking for the two items she sent them after. She pulled out cupcakes, cookies, potato chips, sodas, and sundry candies. The reason is that my father let his grandson, who had no idea what a balanced diet consists of (and to tell the truth he really didn't care), rule him. Marky was driven by his fleshly passion to please his dominant taste for sweets, sweets, and more sweets. Grandpa gave in and helped him. The same happens to us when we get so caught up in the emotions of the moment and the hustle bustle of our everyday activities—

conscious and unconscious—and ignore the needs of our soul. Often, this gradual pattern grows to the point of following the flesh in lockstep fashion, and where it leads us we follow.

We that sow to the flesh get predominantly concerned about fleshly things. Over time, we allow the flesh to guide the general agenda of our lives. And we reap of the flesh many undesirable consequences. However, as we sow to the spirit, we shall of the spirit reap its sweet fruit and life everlasting.

We must keep our minds with all diligence to scripture, prayer, and the Word of God to maintain mastery and dominion over the sensations (the serpents or beasts of the field) of our body. Our souls are obedient to our thoughts and spirit. When we keep our thoughts on God's teachings, purpose, and plan for our lives, His blessings shower us with happiness, harmony, health, wealth, and radiant life.

On the other hand, the surreptitious serpents of sensation stay coiled in our souls, ready to strike when we call forth our attention to such pleasures of the senses as sex, power, envy, jealousy, greed, and willfulness. As we continue to dwell on these temptations, we call forth the willing, waiting, obedient serpent. It stirs, uncoils, takes on an active life force, and energizes its power. It strikes to give pleasure. Left unchecked, the wanton, runaway pleasure of the senses robs the soul and depletes it. We then find ourselves "naked." Seeing our sinfulness, we fall victim to embarrassment, shame, self-condemnation, and guilt. We feel the pain. We see deterioration. Spiritual decay and death are our consequences.

Instead of hiding from God as Adam and Eve did in their nakedness (fleshly nature), we are guided to remember that as God always walked throughout the Garden of Eden instructing Adam, He also walks with us and talks to us today—without ceasing. Just as He called to Adam (life in the body) and Eve (soul), He calls to us (in body, spirit, and soul)—earnestly and tenderly—to keep our hearts and minds turned homeward. He draws us to keep our minds, thoughts, and feelings on God and our God-likeness. He reminds us how He sent his Son Jesus to wipe out the original sin of Adam and Eve to erase the penalty for sin and to obliterate the plague of self-condemnation.

The voice of God runs through our souls as rich and strong as the rivers in Eden to guide our course and renew, refine, and reinvent our desire for God. We are admonished to eliminate the craving to satisfy pleasures of the senses. This restores us to the harmonious relationship destined for our body, soul, and spirit as evidenced by the original Paradise joining Adam (the body), Eve (soul or feeling nature), and the Garden (the wisdom of spirit).

We must continually seek God in the Garden (our eternal bliss) to discover greater aspects of God's love, grace, and goodness. As we seek and search for God's wisdom day and night, without ceasing, God will reveal what He is to us and what we are to Him.

SACRED SCRIPTURE

"So I say, live by the Spirit, and you will not gratify the desires of the sinful nature. For the sinful nature desires what is contrary to the Spirit, and the Spirit what is contrary to the sinful nature. They are in conflict with each other, so that you do not do what you want. But if you are led by the Spirit, you are not under the law."

(Galatians 5:16–18 NIV)

"For what man knoweth the things of a man, save the spirit of man which is in him? . . . Now we have received, not the spirit of the world, but the spirit which is of God. . . ."

(1 Corinthians 2:11–12)

We have received the Spirit of God in our own spirit.

MEDITATION MOMENT

I strive to avoid doing what is wrong and to do what is right in the eyes of God. My soul thirsts for thee, Oh, Lord. I lift my cup to you. Fill it so I might drink of your salvation. I command my flesh to be ruled by the power, authority, and dominion of Jesus Christ. I give thanks to you, Oh Mighty God, for lovingly guiding me to know you, to listen to your words, and to willingly follow your way. I surrender to your Spirit. Amen.

3

✳ A ROUNDABOUT REVELATION

This is a true story. As supernatural or beyond human belief as my story may seem, it is still true. Stay with me as I continue to uncover the mystery of the soul.

From the time I was a child, I have been curious about the soul. I would ask my father, who is a Suffragan Bishop, and my mother, who taught Sunday school for more than 40 years. I asked God to tell me everything I needed to know about the exact location of the soul. I searched high and low for the answer. I sought and sought. I waited and waited. As I waited for God's answer, I thought about it more and then began to ask others. Answers ran the gamut from extensive theological exegesis to biblical hermeneutics. Believers and clergy went to great lengths to pinpoint whether the soul is in the chest area, an area of the brain, or in the "belly." One even said he thought the soul was the heart. A few plainly relented with, "I'm just not sure." or "I don't know."

All these learned men and women of cloth and cloak gave extensive polemical conversation. No one gave me any satisfying food for thought or conviction about my soul and where it is specifically located.

Then I thought, I can't condemn or judge them. When I was a little boy, I was precocious. I was also viewed as a jokester, seeing how I played around a lot. Some concerned people told my mother and father I probably would not live to be sixteen years of age. Even some of my schoolteachers told them the same things. I often wondered why they would say something like that, but now, as I look back, it was probably because they thought if someone else did not kill me for my zany shenanigans, they would. I can't begin to tell you about my ingenuity in pranks, playful plots, and rousing hoaxes. I won't because we must keep our focus on the location of the soul.

As I continued to consider the nature and location of the human soul, I became even more impatient and convinced myself that God would never divulge such valuable information to me. I would stop and wait for God to answer me and then start the round of questioning again: "Lord, where is my soul? Where, oh where?"

Still not hearing the answer, again I looked back on my life and began to feel guilty, and then unworthy. I asked myself, "Who am I to be asking God where my soul is?" I grew even more weary when I recalled how pastors, church members, Sunday School teachers, my parents' houseguests, and my church peers described the soul as a precious possession, the seat of affection, the great abyss, "the unknowable," or as in the popular spaghetti sauce saying—"it's in there somewhere." I knew it was in there, but "where?" I grew introspective. As I meditated, I whispered from the depth of my heart, "God, please tell me where."

There was a lull and a hush. Jesus Christ began to show me that I was worthy for Him to shape my understanding of the nature and location of the human soul. He reminded me that He died for my sins. He spread a panorama before me displaying His goodness in my life such as the gift of water baptism at the tender age of seven and claiming the infilling of the Holy Spirit at the age of nine. Then, as a preacher's kid, I served as a drummer for the choir, youth leader, bus driver, lawn boy, cook, pop machine attendant, song service leader, altar worker, and pianist. Little did I know then that these—and later serving as traveling evangelist, church board member, Assistant Pastor, and a community leader—were preparing me for the church ministry as a multimedia evangelist, Suffragan Bishop, and pastor of a congregation of more than 2,000.

God Works in Mysterious Ways

When He laid out my practiced virtues, personal sacrifice, spiritual gifts, evangelism, and other selfless services in plain view before me, a rush of tears streamed down my cheeks. I cried, "Yes, Lord, I am worthy to hear your answer. I am ready like I never knew before to understand any and everything you have to tell me about the soul. You can trust me to hear and understand you, trust you, and teach others about their souls." I felt a sudden shift. It was like a quickening, followed by an outpouring of blessings from heaven into my very soul. I had finally heard from the Lord, and He told me He would answer me in His own time. I inhaled deeply and then exhaled thoroughly, releasing all concerns, anxieties, and worries about my answer. I accepted God's timing and chimed in with, " Lord, I surrender to your Will and your way for me to know about the soul." I felt assured as I settled down and hummed a song my mother taught me when I was a little boy, "You'll Understand It Better By and By."

A year later, I heard God's answer. I was driving from Chicago, Illinois, to Clinton, Iowa, to minister with my sister and her husband who were laboring in a three-month church ministry. The Lord had led me to bless their new ministry with time and talent—without accepting any payment for my service. I also took them a monetary offering. My soul did not want the bumpy ride of a prop plane to Clinton, Iowa. So I flew to Chicago, rented a car, and drove to Clinton. On the way, I was constantly talking to God. I often keep a running conversation with God as I drive my own car along city streets, rural routes, and interstate freeways.

As I talked with excitement and animation, I felt a flutter of constraint. I quickly recovered when I thought about people driving down the street smoking, and they are not ashamed. I had a flashback to stereo speakers filling up the rear view and back seat of young people's cars. As they blast the entire neighborhood with the beat of deafening hip-hop and rap, they're not ashamed. Then I thought, no one can see whom I'm talking to, but I know to whom I am talking.

I kept repeating: I know Jesus is real. I know Jesus is alive and well, and I know He is in this car with me right now. So I am not going to be concerned about the folks who might think I'm crazy. I'm just going to keep talking to my invisible, yet tangible passenger. Then I invoked my spirit of praise in the car.

The praises to God began to flow freely from my mouth. My lips moved almost uncontrollably, and I added vigorous hand gestures as I praised and magnified my Lord. I am sure it looked like I was talking on my hands-free car phone, but I was talking to God. I was thanking Him, worshipping Him, and rejoicing in His glory. We were having first-fruits fellowship. I praised God with, "Lord, I bless your name. Your name alone is excellent. Your power is awesome. Your ways are not my ways. Your riches are unending, your power is unconquerable, and your love for humanity is beyond my ability to even begin to comprehend."

When Our Praises Go Up, Blessings Flow

The more I praised God, the more He responded to my praise. My praises grew louder and louder, stronger and stronger. I could feel God's love resonating with my heart. The lub-dub of the Holy Spirit regulated the melody in my spirit and my soul. I could hardly contain myself in the spirited enclosure of my car. As tears filled my eyes, I turned on the windshield wipers. Although it was raining outside, I was also aware of the Holy Spirit "reigning" inside the car.

As I worshiped God, the Shekinah Glory consumed my body, spirit, and soul. The joy of the living Lord filled my car. This confirmed what I already knew—wherever we send up praises, God meets us there. God met me so strongly on that isolated two-lane country road on the way to Clinton, Iowa, I had to pull off the road to further commune with Him. I heard the distinct voice of God. At that point, I was not even consciously concerned about the location of my soul. I was caught up in high praise and worship of my King (King Jesus), my Savior, and the Lover of my soul. With praises ebbing, tears still flowing, and the joy of the Lord prevailing, the sweet sacred anointing of God lingered like lilac throughout my car. I felt energized and renewed.

God's Spirit fell like the morning glory through the grayish colored skies of that rainy day. He whispered into my innermost being, "Do you really want to know where your soul is?"

I sat up straight in my seat and framed my fresh face in the rear view mirror. It was I. I pinched myself and asked, "Is this real? Was that the voice I had so longed to hear?"

I felt like a child on Christmas morning after staying awake on Christmas Eve night, waiting and waiting. I felt like a child who had been begging his parents for his most ardent desire or plaything, and his parents had not said no, because they just did not see that as the time to give it. But on that day it was like my parents decided to give me that thing I so deeply yearned for.

I wish you could have seen the wide-eyed look on my wet, tear-filled face when the Lord finally came and placed the climactic answer in my ears and heart. I cried, "Hallelujah! Thank you, God." The answer may not have come when I, the child in spirit, wanted it, but it came when I had matured enough to receive it. Although elated, I stayed humble to receive God's revelation. I whispered softly, "Yes, Lord."

The Answer

Sunshine broke through the clouds. I rejoiced, stepped outside the rental car, stretched, got back behind the wheel, and drove on to Clinton. God began to share with me the location of the soul and His sacredness in the whole matter. It was God's Word found in a very familiar passage of Scripture that all preachers have exhorted at one time or another in their ministries. But in order to get the real meaning, I must tell you about how the revelation unfolded on the rest of my trip to Clinton. As you read, I pray that you truly grasp it because it is a deep knowledge from God, according to the Scripture.

Back on the Road Again

Every mile along the route, God's inspired word helped me see His plan and promise regarding the soul. As His revelation unraveled, the location of the soul became plain to me. You see, the road to Clinton was bucolic. Farmland seemed to stretch far beyond the horizon. Cows grazed. Bulls dozed. Goats played. Sheep rallied together. Wheat and grain grew and stretched across countless acres. Red barns and tall silos positioned themselves strategically among the farms and fields.

God showed me how each figure and form symbolized something significant. He painted in my mind's eye the sacred scenes from the great Jewish feasts including Passover, Pentecost, and Tabernacles. Then He reminded me of the lesser feasts—Trumpets, Dedication, and Purim. He showed me the symbolism in the Day of Atonement—also known to us as Yom Kippur. This Levital ritual was not a feast day, but a day of fasting and penitence which was practiced by the Jews in the wilderness the tenth day of the seventh month (September in the Babylonian Calendar). We learn from Leviticus 16 that on this "holiest day" special animals (e.g., goats, rams, and bullock) were offered as sin and burnt offerings to cleanse the Jews "from all sin before the Lord" (atone for sins). This was practiced by the Israelites once a year, with the high priest also atoning for the altar, the holy sanctuary, and the Israelites.

These symbols signify meaning for us today. Jesus was crucified at the time of Passover. Today, we know Him as "the Lamb of God, which takes away the sins of the world." The church began its work at Pentecost. The feast of Tabernacles reminds us of America's Thanksgiving Day and the early days when American Indians and white men and women celebrated the abundance of harvest. God began to show me how these symbols and many more from this scenic rural route to Clinton, Iowa, relate to the location of the soul. With high expectancy, I drove on.

4

✸ The Scene and Unseen

As I continued the drive to Clinton, fertile crops kept coming into full view and then fading in the distance—one after the other. Any recapturing came from a quick glance in my rearview mirror. The passing barns and fields reminded me of the Feast of the Tabernacle (Feast of Ingathering) which commemorated the years the Israelites wandered in the wilderness and lived in temporary booths or tents in the fields where their crops grew (Leviticus 23). This feast was held the fifteenth day of the seventh month (October in our calendar). It was a celebration of final harvest when the first fruits (harvests) of the year had been gathered in. The Israelites also gathered in oil and wine.

As God continued to focus my spiritual lenses, my awareness of God's fulfillment and promises sharpened. The vision of the tabernacle during the time of the Day of Atonement and the Feast of the Tabernacle appeared before me in clear view. Eureka!

God's Perfect Pattern

When the Hebrews were delivered from the bondage of Pharaoh in Egypt, they were ready to begin their new life as an independent nation. Whereas America began its independent nation with the Declaration of Independence and the Constitution, Moses brought law, order, and interdependence through the God-revealed commandments given at Mount Sinai. God also gave specific, unalterable instructions for building a tabernacle. This was to be a symbol for God's dwelling among His people. It was to serve as a center of worship.

The Hebrew word for tabernacle is transliterated to the common word for "tent." The tabernacle was to be God's tent in the midst of the tents of his people. Just as tents were temporary and could be taken down and moved as the nomadic Hebrews made their way through the wilderness toward the Promised Land, so could the tabernacle. God's sacred and specific instructions for building the tabernacle were spelled out in the minutest detail. And as He gave them to Moses, He warned him to follow them flawlessly.

> *Tabernacle* [Tab/ ur nak/ ul]—tent or a temporary dwelling which served as a place of worship for the nation of Israel during their early history. It was a portable sanctuary and used after the commandments, judgments, and ordinances given by God to Moses for the building of the temple in Jerusalem by Solomon.

The construction of the tabernacle along with its fine furnishings and architecture is described verbatim in Exodus, chapters 35 through 40. You can read about all of the glorious, ornate patterns for this heavenly center of worship, praise, prayer, and sacrifice at your leisure. However, to help you see a glimpse of God's skillful hand at work, join me as we tour this costly, yet sacred ornate structure (estimated at some $1,250,000).[1]

Outer Court

The Outer Court (sometimes referred to as "yard") that surrounded and fenced in the tabernacle was rectangular and measured 150 feet long by 75 feet wide. The Outer Court faced east. It was constructed with "hangings of fine twined linen, seven and one-half feet high, on pillars of brass (standing) seven and one-half feet apart, with fillets and hooks of silver, set in sockets of brass."[2] The gate providing entrance into the court (at the east end) measured 30 feet wide. It was draped with blue and scarlet linen and was the only doorway in or out of the courtyard.

Altar of Burnt Offering

Immediately after entering the Court one would approach the altar of burnt offering and the laver (on the east side). Looking farther to the west end of the court, one could see the tabernacle. The altar of burnt offering (standing east of the tabernacle) was seven and one-half feet square, and four and one-half feet high. This was the great altar for sacrificing animals. Built of durable acacia boards, the altar was covered with brass and was hollow. It was to be filled with earth. The ledge, extending halfway up, provided a step for priests to stand on for their Levitical rituals. The fire on the altar was constantly kindled and miraculously never went out.

The Laver

The laver stood west of the altar of burnt offering and just west of the tabernacle. This large brass basin held water for priests to wash their hands and feet before ministering at the altar, before entering the tent (tabernacle).

The Building

The tabernacle building was designed in the form of a tent, 45 feet long, 15 feet wide, and 15 feet high. It was set up with only one entrance at the east end. It was the only way in and out of the tent. The tent covering consisted of a wooden framework made of 46 identical planks, 45 feet long and two feet, three inches wide. Twenty planks supported the north and south sides. Six of the planks were on the west end, along with two additional planks, which were three inches wide. All the planks were the strong durable acacia wood, plated with gold. Each had two tenons at one end, to be stood upright on two sockets of silver, and held together with five bars running through golden rings on the boards.

The Roof

The curtain, four separate coverings, made up the roof of the structure. The first covering was made of fine-twined linen of blue, scarlet, and purple with intricately portrayed cherubim. The second covering was of pure white goat's hair. The third was of ram's skins dyed red. The topmost covering was of material referred to in the King James Version of the Bible as badger skins. Some American translations of the Bible suggest that this should be translated porpoise skins, or possibly leather.

Two Rooms

The tabernacle constructed in this manner was then divided into two rooms; each separated by an intricate veil of blue, scarlet, and purple linen embroidered with cherubim. The outer eastern room was named the **Holy Place** and inner or western room the **Most Holy Place** or **Holy of Holies.** The entire curtain (formed by ten curtains) was 60 feet east and west, 42 feet north and south and an extra 15 feet to hang over the west end. This whole curtain (made of a total of ten curtains) covered the tabernacle proper.

Holy Place

The Holy Place (the outer eastern room) was the first point of entry into the tent (tabernacle). One passed through a screen (or veil) made of fine blue, purple, and scarlet linen, at the east end of the tabernacle. This was the only doorway for entrance to or exit from the tabernacle. The Holy Place measured 30 by 15 feet. It contained three sacred items—the Table of Shewbread, on the north side, the candlestick on the south side, and the Altar of Incense just before the inner veil (separating the Holy Place and the Most Holy Place). The Table of Shewbread, three feet long by one and one-half feet wide by two and one-quarter feet high, was made of the finest, strongest acacia wood, overlaid with pure gold. It held twelve loaves of bread which were replaced anew each Sabbath.

Candlestick

The candlestick was made of pure gold with a central shaft and three branches on each side. It was five feet high and three and one-half feet across the top. Fed with olive oil, it was trimmed and lit daily. The candlestick gave light to the Holy Place.

Altar of Incense

The Altar of Incense stood three feet high and measured one and one-half feet square. Incense was to be burned on the Altar of Incense morning and evening (Exodus 30:8). Made of the durable acacia wood and overlaid with pure gold, the Altar of Incense commanded its sacred position to the west of the veil (exquisitely embroidered cherubim and made with only the finest blue, purple, and scarlet linen) that separated the Holy Place and the Most Holy Place (or Holy of Holies).

God's Knowledge Revealed

Pause with me as we take a close look at this part of God's revelation. This is the crowning point of God's perfect construction and marks unequivocal, matchless architecture—the **Most Holy Place,** or **Holy of Holies.** As I thought on this, it was as though heaven's windows, doors, and screens opened to the choirs of angels as they sang in sonata form. They vibrated to the trumpets as they sounded a glorious clarion call to the body of

Christ to praise and worship our Lord and Savior Jesus Christ. I felt a rising of the Holy Spirit within me and throughout my body and soul. I began to sing and shout praises to the Lord—Hallelujah! Glory to God! Thanks be to God! What a mighty God we serve!

The Holy of Holies

The Holy of Holies (or Most Holy Place), a perfect cube (fifteen feet long, wide, and high) constructed on the west end of the tabernacle, represented God's dwelling place. It contained only the Ark of the Covenant. It was a wooden chest (three and three-fourths feet long, two and one-fourth feet wide, and two and one-fourth feet high) covered with gold and topped with a golden lid (called the Mercy Seat) bearing two golden cherubim. The cherubim faced each other. The Ark was the most sacred of all sacred structures because in it were Aaron's rod that budded (God's power), the two tables of the Ten Commandments (God's government), and a Pot of Manna (God's providence). Only the high priest was allowed to enter the Holy of Holies, and this was once a year during the Day of Atonement ritual.

God's Rich Supply

All the gold and silver used in the construction of the tabernacle and in the supply of its furnishings came from the treasures given by the Egyptians (Exodus 12:35). They were estimated at more than $1,250,000.[3] Only God could show such a hand in the beyond-human, beyond-belief miracle of the original tabernacle. I still marvel at His mighty power, intelligence, and dominion over all creation.

Continuing to Clinton

As I continued the drive into Clinton, Iowa, grinning from ear to ear and burning with excitement from head to foot about

God's revelation, I spotted a car passing in the opposite direction. The male driver was grinning and waving to me. What he didn't know was that I was not smiling at him. But that was okay because smiles are contagious. It would be wonderful if everyone would spread some sunshine every day to brighten, lighten, and lift our spirits.

God was not finished. He said, "Mark, that was only an eye-opener. I want to show you something that will expand your knowledge about the soul and its location." I knew that I would not be able to keep the car on the road or avoid an accident as God dealt with me this next time. I looked at my watch and saw I was making good time in my ground travel. As I pulled off the road again, I rejoiced and thanked God for safe, blessed, and anointed traveling. I thanked Him for His inspired Word and His revelation about the soul. I parked the car, turned off the ignition, bowed my head, and prayed. God's presence filled the car and my soul.

SACRED SCRIPTURE

"Know ye not that ye are the temple of God, and that the Spirit of God dwelleth in you? If any man defile the temple of God, him shall God destroy; for the temple of God is holy, which temple ye are."

(1 Corinthians 3:16–17)

MEDITATION MOMENT

As I think on God's magnificence, I know I am a temple of the living God. I choose to love my body temple as God loves me. I treat my body temple as a clean and holy dwelling for the Spirit of God to work His perfect plan in and through my life. God's providence, presence, and power prevailing for me lead, guide, and direct me in all my ways. I continually seek God's guidance.

Thank you, God, for revealing your love, grace, mercy, and tender loving care to my body temple. I willingly follow you on my path to growing in your Spirit. Amen.

5

✸ Enter Ye

As I was ready to finish my prayer with "Amen," I listened for God's guidance. He inserted, "What I just showed you about the tabernacle was a mere beginning. You saw only physical formations and biblical symbols. Now I want to take you to another level of knowledge about the soul—to signs, meanings, and true answers to remove the mystery about the soul. I will show you practical applications. I want to show you spiritual discernment for the soul."

Feeling privileged, I could hardly contain myself. I felt confident about where God was about to take me and what He was about to show me about the human soul. I knew it would be discernible, yet clear. It would be comprehensive, yet comprehensible.

I opened my laptop, booted it up, and began to process notes as fast as my fingers would function. As I released personal ego and let go of any need to lean on my own knowledge and intelligence, I allowed God to teach me the unfiltered and unadulterated truth about the location of the soul.

God revealed the signs and meanings about the tabernacle and humankind at physical, spiritual, and soul levels. As He continued to command my spirit with His revelation, I entered commands on my keyboard at what seemed faster than nanosecond speed. New understanding shaped new wisdom, and new wisdom formed new ideas about the soul. These God inspired ideas evoked new spiritual discernment. As I followed the guidance of the Holy Spirit, I listened, learned, and wrote from God's inspiration for more than three hours. He revealed the *soul*.

This struck the new beginning of profound knowledge and deeper understanding God had promised me. This continual revelation lasted long after I returned home from this trip. Through fervent prayer, fasting, and praising God for new understanding and wisdom about the location of the soul, He revealed more and more. I continued to search and research for about seven years after the Clinton trip, and, to no surprise, God continued to bless my quest with countless resources to help reveal the mysteries of the soul.

Just at the right times He led me to appropriate Scriptures, personal lessons, and spiritual revivals about the soul. He sent evangelists, prophets, pastor, peers, Bible scholars, and His direct communication and revelation.

God showed me how He creates new awareness of His wisdom, how He clarifies understanding, and how He causes humankind to discern Truth. He reveals the meanings in patterns; however, in His own time in history and in our own experiences as we are ready. God knows our readiness for revelation, and His patterns are pure and perfect as fine-cut flawless diamonds—clear-cut, lucid, and luminous.

As we seek God's answers through our prayers, spiritual discernment, and praise, He shows us His fine works, the meanings, and the messages in the patterns of His creations. When He sees that we have reached the state of readiness, He does not hide His Will, His Word, or His revelation from us. The Holy Spirit showed me the distinct patterns in the systematic unfoldment of His creation of "man," the fall of man, the redemption of man, the forty years of wanderings of Moses and the Israelites in the wilderness, and the building of the perfect tabernacle. This helped me see, and to later show others, the magnificent handiwork of God for His people in past times, today, and forevermore.

From Symbols to Meaning

But we must constantly seek Him to know Him and His patterns for gaining spiritualized intellect, knowledge, understanding, wisdom, and discernment. We must rest on the assurance of God's promise to us, assuring that as we ask, seek, and knock on the door of God's presence, He answers and gives liberally to our requests. How this involved discourse on God's patterns relates to the location of the soul is that the structure of the physical human-made tabernacle relates to the trichotomy of humankind—body, spirit, and soul.

Just as the tabernacle served the Israelites as a complete, distinct, and perfect whole, we are a complete whole unit in body, spirit, and soul. From a spiritual viewpoint, humankind contains an "outer court," a holy place, and a most holy place (holy of holies). The *outer court* represents the human body. The *holy place* represents the human spirit and the *most holy place* (holy of holies) represents the soul of humankind. The body, spirit, and soul make up our temple of the living God. And the spirit of God dwells in our body, spirit, and soul. We are created to live holy even as God, our creator and maker, is holy.

A brief revisit to the tabernacle will enable us to see this pattern more clearly. I will review the pattern at three levels—*physical, spiritual,* and *soul.*

The Meaning and Message within the Tabernacle		
Outer Court	**Holy Place**	**Most Holy Place**
Yard about the Tabernacle	Outer Tent (larger part)	Inner Tent (smaller part)
Place of Sacrifice for the World	Place of Worship	Place of Sacrifice and Spiritual Communion with God
Body (flesh)	Human Spirit	Human Soul

Let's examine the "tabernacle" at the *soul* level. The human soul is twined with the human spirit. As spirit and soul are intertwined (interlocked or enfolded together), they are "locked up" in the body to express through the body temple (the outer) in a likewise manner (looking alike as twins). As such, the soul expresses from spirit. Also, the body (outer) expresses as spirit and soul express (inner)—"soul like me."

The soul resides in our temple (body) along with our spirit. Dwelling with the human spirit and soul is the Spirit of God (1 Corinthians 3:16). As our human spirit follows the leading, guiding, teaching, and feeding of the Holy Spirit, our soul follows likewise—as within (spirit and soul), so without (body).

A Case in Point

A few years ago a believer came to me for spiritual counseling. He described his long bout with rheumatoid arthritis while growing up from a little boy to adolescence. Apparently, his father's mother lived with his family of nine to help out in their dual-career family, with his father and mother working long hours and traveling with their jobs.

Around the house, his grandmother did it all—washed and ironed clothes, scrubbed floors, shopped for groceries, cooked the meals, and bathed the babies. She was a stern taskmaster and ruled the roost stricter than General George Smith Patton, Jr. ruled the cavalry.

While an adolescent, bad grew to worse when his rheumatoid arthritis advanced to the crippling stage. However, he recovered fully one year after his grandmother died. He believes it was because he was no longer under the stress and strain of her matriarchal rule.

He came to see me because, in his early adulthood, the arthritis had returned to his body. This time as the deadly lupus. He saw himself as a victim in an abusive marriage. His wife was bipolar, a chronic hypochondriac, and unsaved (a nonbeliever). Feeling desolate, dispirited, and desperate, he saw divorce or suicide as his only solution. He wanted to remove himself from his painful, dysfunctional marriage and from life. I thought on the Word of God:

> *Beloved, I wish above all things that thou mayest prosper and be in health, even as thy soul prospereth.*
>
> —3 John, second verse

The NIV reads:

> *Dear friend, I pray that you may enjoy good health and that all may go well with you, even as your soul is getting along well.*

This man's compelling story lucidly shows how both the hidden spirit and soul locked up in the body become known, apparent, and eventually outwardly expressed through the body, visibly and luminously. Other visible manifestations evidenced by the outward expression (body) of the inner soul and spirit: "a red face" or blushing, shingles, and hives, to name just a few. These manifest visibly through the observable outer skin of the body, but stem from the inner expressions of the invisible spirit and soul. This means that the soul is twined with the spirit, and the issues of soul and spirit express and manifest observably through the body. The body reveals the "soul like you." It is therefore essential to:

> *Keep thy heart with all diligence* [guard or watch]; *for out of it are the issues of life.*
>
> —Proverbs 4:23

Spirit and Soul

God breathed His Spirit into humankind to give life, order, and unity to all bodily functions. The Holy Spirit fortifies the soul and prepares it for eternal life with God.

The soul is located next to human spirit to be led, guided, impressed, and inspired by the spirit. As our human spirit obeys the direct guidance of the Holy Spirit and *responds inkind,* the soul—intertwined with our own spirit—acts likewise.

Also, when the human spirit does not yield to the Spirit of God, the soul *responds inkind* and acts likewise. Our soul acts from our spirit, whether through choosing to act from the Spirit of God or by our own personal will to make wrong choices caused by the rule of flesh. The spirit leads the soul, and the soul then responds in-kind as on automatic pilot, answering to human spirit. It does only what it is told or acted upon to do by our human spirit.

Our soul doesn't think, reason, or question. It responds as automatically as the gearshift on a car is manipulated when we drive a standard gearshift. It does only what we press on it to do as we shift from gear to gear (from human decision to decision).

Likewise, the body shows on the outer what is going on in the inner (spirit and soul). As I shared earlier in this chapter, when our spirit is obedient to the Holy Spirit and follows the teaching of the Word of God, our soul becomes "Holy Spirit fed and led," and we show up visibly and observably as peaceful, joyful, and made "every whit" whole. Our spirit and soul are intertwined and are reflected as a mirror through the visible, outwardly observable body.

Obeying the Holy Spirit takes our trust in Its power, dominion, and authority in our lives and in all living things. Also, obedience requires our vigilant awareness to "keep our spirit and soul" with all diligence and attention to the Holy Spirit (meditating on Him day and night). This is how we can get victory over sin, sickness, and affliction.

The soul is eternal. It lives on after the death of the physical body. Thus, the soul will live eternally after its temporary stay on earth.

The Soul Lives On and On

Let's look at the situation between Lazarus (the "beggar") and the rich ruler as found in Luke 16:19-31. (Read this passage in your Bible.) Notice in Luke 16:22 the writer proclaims that both men die. Lazarus is carried into Abraham's bosom by the angels and the rich ruler is buried and later lifts up his eyes in Sheol-Hades (a temporary abode of the souls of the wicked dead). Both men die, and both have a soul that has to dwell somewhere in eternity.

So, look at what happens. The rich man desires a sip of cool water and asks the same man he had refused to feed (which ultimately caused him to lose his life) to get him some water. "Some nerve," you might say. I do not want to argue whether getting him some water was the correct thing to do. The salient point is how did the rich man recognize Lazarus?

It is evident in the Scriptures that no flesh shall inherit eternal life. We must believe in the Word of God. It's true.

> *Now this I say, brethren, that flesh and blood cannot inherit the kingdom of God; neither doth corruption inherit incorruption.*
>
> —1 Corinthians 15:50

So, in Luke 16:22, the rich man's body was buried in a grave. Also, Lazarus was buried in a grave. Both men knew each other on the earth plane. One was rich and the other (Lazarus) was poor. The soul of the rich man definitely knew what Lazarus looked like on earth in soul form. Now he recognized him beyond the earth. As I pointed out earlier, the Scripture says the rich man was transported to Sheol-Hades. Lazarus was ushered to Paradise which is separated from Sheol-Hades by a gulf.

The key to operating knowledge about your soul: The outer shell or layer of the body person represents the flesh of humankind. The second layer is the spirit. The third, more inner layer, is the soul. All three take on the same shape, same image, and the same likeness.

However, bear in mind what Scriptures spell out regarding dividing asunder body, spirit, and soul:

> *The word of God is quick, and powerful, and sharper than any twoedged sword, piercing even to the dividing asunder of soul and spirit, and the joints of the marrow, and is a discerner of the thoughts and intents of the heart.*
>
> —Hebrews 4:12

At death, God takes the spirit and soul into His custody, and only God can operate on the soul and the spirit. The writer of Hebrews, inspired by God, points out that just as sure as there is a separation between bone and marrow (body) there is also a separation between soul and spirit when one dies.

Now, I ask you, "How did the rich man recognize Lazarus?"

Both were physically dead. Both were dispatched to eternal destinations—Lazarus in the bosom of Abraham (place of eternal blessedness) and the rich ruler in Sheol-Hades (place of eternal torment). The only way one could have recognized the other is that the *soul* of humankind looks just like the outer man when it goes on to its eternal dwelling place. So, I have coined a phrase: "The real me is 'locked up inside my flesh,' and the real me lives beyond the grave."

Remember that our eternal soul has feelings, emotions, and personality. And, most important, it lives forever. Inside you stands the soul: a woman or man that looks just like you, and, in essence, is the "real you" (your soul). This is the entwined you (your twin) that expresses inside you as you. This is a pattern established by God—yesterday, today, and forevermore. This is true revelation from the Word of God. Seek it. See it. Believe it. Act faithfully on it because *how* you govern your outer person's manifestation and expression in this lifetime determines *where* your inner person (your "twin") spends eternity.

From that time, God has continued to reveal knowledge about the "entwined spirit and soul" and the mirror image on the body. I continue to live in utter awe about this perfect pattern. When you look in the mirror, the face or full body that you see is the temporary you. The temporary you is your flesh.

However, in this family united in body, spirit, and soul, your flesh tries to rule the permanent or eternal you—your soul. You must not allow this. It is time to place your spirit under the yoke of the Holy Spirit that seeks to rest, rule, guide, and rightly divide fact from fiction. The Holy Spirit abides within you to continuously heal your infirmities. It works to empower you against the flesh and all evil.

When you allow the Holy Spirit to rule and work in your spirit, you help to renew, revive, and regenerate your soul. You restore your soul to abide in the Paradise of God forever.

SACRED SCRIPTURE

"Take my yoke upon you, and learn of me; for I am meek and lowly in heart: and ye shall find rest unto your souls. For my yoke is easy, and my burden is light."

(Matthew 11:29–30)

MEDITATION MOMENT

The Holy Spirit leads me and guides me in all ways that are as His image and likeness. I commit my life to God and willingly follow Him in all my thoughts, words, deeds, and actions. My spirit is led and fed by the Holy Spirit. My body, spirit, and soul reflect the perfect pattern of God's Will. His love and grace supply my soul with satisfaction and sufficiency. My soul's quest is to dwell in the House of the Lord forever.

Thank you, Jesus, for loving my soul so much as to save it from eternal destruction. My soul magnifies the Lord. Amen.

6

✴ The War Is On

After ending the soul revelation sojourn on my drive from Chicago, Illinois, to Clinton, Iowa, (to minister in my brother-in-law's church ministry), I felt physically exhausted, yet inspired in spirit by the new knowledge God revealed to me about the soul. Sitting in my parked car, I pressed my tired shoulders against the smooth leather of the driver's seat. Sheer exhaustion quickly ushered me into a deep nap.

A series of rapid-fire pecking on the window of my car shocked me to an awakened state. As I looked to my left, I made eye contact with a fellow driver as he pressed his face to my car window. "Need some help?" he asked. I smiled at him and answered, "Everything's fine. Thanks for checking." Satisfied, he slowly walked away. As I peered through my side view mirror, I watched him as he returned to his car. Feeling fully awake by now, I inhaled deeply. As I exhaled, I felt a new zest for life, living, and giving.

God had given me loads of fresh insight and new perspective. I said out loud, "This is the day the Lord made. I will rejoice and be glad in it." The remaining drive to Clinton flew by like a flash. I rejoiced and, as I would with my best friend, talked with God until I turned into my sister's driveway in Clinton.

While ministering in Clinton, God helped me serve in more ways than I had planned. Through God's guidance and anointing, I was able to bless the church ministry far beyond previous expectations. Most important was the saving of souls.

Come into His Presence

Now, back to the present time in understanding the soul. I have lots more to share with you about your soul. In a biblical, yet practical way, I will show you how to care for your soul, edify your soul, and save your soul from eternal damnation.

The remaining chapters of this book address these essential elements (caring, edifying, saving) that work together for a healthy, satisfied soul. These spirited chapters will minister to your precious soul. As you read, you will find more answers to your burning questions and critical concerns about your soul. You will find powerful antidotes, more sacred Scriptures, true testimonials, and practical applications about the soul. Most of all, you will be inspired and motivated to take action on what God intends for you to do about your soul. As you do, you will enjoy your satisfied soul.

The Flesh and the Spirit

The spirit is willing to do what is right, but the flesh is weak. The Apostle Paul, whom many say was the greatest man in the Bible, apart from Jesus, said of himself,

> *For that which I do I allow [know] not: for what*
> *I would do, that do I not; but what I hate, that*
> *do I. For I know that in me [that is, in my flesh]*
> *dwelleth no good thing: for to will is present*
> *with me; but how to perform that which is good*
> *I find not.*
>
> —Romans 7:15, 18

This is not to say that we should pattern the wars between the states of our flesh and spirit as Paul did, but more so to show you an example of what each one of us faces on our soul's journey to attain victory over our flesh. When we would do "good," the evil one (flesh) vies for its victories within us. We have only one soul and one spirit, and both flesh and spirit stay in a constant tug of war to win our attention. We might say that the war is on the inside, but the war is as much external as it is internal.

The war is between the temporary yes and the eternal yes. It's between the present perks and pleasures that last for a short present time and long-term future rewards—those things that are eternal in God (joy, peace, life, love). Galatians 5:17 points out:

> *For the flesh lusteth against the Spirit, and the Spirit against the flesh: and these are contrary the one to the other: so that ye cannot do the things that ye would.*

The word "contrary" means to lie opposite or to oppose. The flesh opposes the spirit and soul as much as the serpent opposed the good and pure spirit of Eve in the Garden (before The Fall). In us dwell both the spirit of humankind and the Spirit of life. We cannot see our spirit, so we sometimes ask, "Where is the war?"

The war is between the flesh and the spirit. The flesh seeks to be the captain of the spirit. Peter exhorts us to "Be sober, be vigilant; because your adversary the devil, as a roaring lion, walketh about, seeking whom he may devour" (1 Peter 5:8). The flesh is fighting every day to take control of your thoughts, decisions, and circumstances in your life. Your flesh seeks to disobey the commands of the Holy Spirit and to drive you to that which is wrong in God's eyes—disobedience and unethical, sinful desires. Obviously, these do not work for your good. No good thing dwells in your flesh.

Flesh seeks to tell you the *why*, the *when*, and the *where* that have to be sought after and answered on your quest to obey God's commandments. Flesh is relentless in its quest to overrule the spirit. James 4:1 challenges us with, "From whence come wars and fighting among you? Come they not hence, even of your lusts that war in your members?" Further in his letter James admonishes with "submit yourselves to God. Resist the devil, and he will flee from you" (James 4:7). You must be vigilant with the flesh and do daily battle. It is "no more nice guys" when you are dealing with flesh.

Protecting Your Soul

I have found that people will get into fist fights and arguments over some of the most trivial things. When I investigate or inquire more specifically, I discover the root cause stems from one of the lusts—of the flesh or of the eye or one of the prides of life. The power of the personal ego and one of the *self*-things such as selfishness, *self*-delusion, *self*-centeredness, *self*-sufficiency, *self*-pity, or *self*-defense will cause people to attack and fight each other. Unfortunately, they find little time for self-examination.

When we use self-inspection and self-insight, we fight flesh by exposing the darkness to the light of God for clarity. This guiding light leads us to take a realistic look at the fight that is going on outside and within. Over time, we find that the fight is more within the members of our own mind and body than forces outside, such as those of the other person.

An even closer inspection will show that the flesh sides with that which satisfies the flesh, and does not account for what will hurt or destroy. False pride, arrogance, haughtiness, disobedience, and defensiveness will weaken your spirit and eventually take you down. As a result, you will make decisions to your own destruction—physically, emotionally, and spiritually.

Peter pleads and implores us to "abstain from fleshly lusts which war against the soul" (1 Peter 2:11). Remember: The fleshly lust seeks to destroy the soul. Every time the flesh "chalks up" another strike for eternal damnation, it is victorious and we fail to protect the soul. When we allow this over a long period, we lose our soul to the devil.

How many times has your unruly flesh caused you to make decisions that hurt you? What was the root cause? What did you do about it?

A Case in Point

A believer once confessed to me how she failed to protect her soul and described the life-threatening consequences. She showed guilt and embarrassment as she began to talk about it. After I prayed for her, she calmed down and began to tell her story.

Before she was saved, her wanton life looked as if it was racing at top speed on a downhill ski slope. She said that turning to Christ prevented her from smashing head first into what seemed like "a daunting pine tree three-quarters of the way to the bottom of the steep slope." She was determined to stay saved.

After practicing celibacy for almost ten years (she was saved during that time), she met her "prince charming." She said his convincing style was smoother than silk and more slippery than any serpent in Adam and Eve's Garden. He knew just what to say as he whispered the right kind and tender words. He knew when to turn on his disarming smile and where to target the endearing twinkle from his big brown eyes—right to the center of her loving heart and soul. He showered her with the penultimate of politeness and polish. He held back no measure of sweetness. With lust "burning in her loins," she could not resist him or restrain her unruly flesh.

To no avail, she prayed and fasted for complete deliverance. Lust soon inflamed her. Later, it engulfed her entire body. Flesh was on the rampage and was raging out of control—worse than a northern California forest fire. She said she "left herself wide open" for the subtle serpent. It slid into her thoughts with: "Surely one sleepover can't hurt. He's such a nice guy."

As much as the Holy Spirit warned her, admonished her, and showed her the error of her prevailing sexual desires, she acquiesced to error and had a sexual affair (fornication). The next week he proposed.

Without praying about her decision or allowing the Holy Spirit to guide her spirit (and save her soul), she answered, "Yes." The man she married was a nonbeliever and had never been saved. This beautiful, yet misguided woman, said that her lust and out of control flesh forced her hand. Flesh preempted the "goodness" of her spirit to make a bad decision that caused deep pain and profound sadness in her life for more than ten years. Bad grew to worse.

She discovered that her husband engaged in and supported several extramarital affairs and passed on a sexually transmitted disease to her. He drained her bank account and investment portfolio bone dry. After there was no more to take from her, he wanted out. He abandoned her and filed for divorce. She was devastated.

Dispirited and spiritually destroyed, she stood naked before God. Feeling embarrassed and guilty, she was sure that God would strike her dead and cast her into the lake of fire forever. Instead, God's grace prevailed. He inclined His ear to her as she asked God to forgive her. Weeping for what seemed like nonstop, she expressed deep, godly sorrow for her sins. She repented, was led back to Christ, and reclaimed her soul. She felt a close relatedness with Christ, more than ever before.

Unruly Flesh Destroys

Countless times church members and walk-in counselees have confessed their out-of-control, runaway fleshly desires. Most involve situations of sex, power, manipulation, and money. The destructive works of unchecked flesh pushed these people to pornography, fornication, adultery, eating disorders, substance abuse, workaholism, fraud, grand larceny, gambling addiction, alcoholism, and mental illness—to name only a few. Many ended up divorced, unemployed, bankrupt, hospitalized, or incarcerated.

Unchecked flesh destroys at every level. It creates problems in one's personal life, at work, in one's career, in the family, and in the church. It destroys body, soul, and spirit. And I continue to ask, "What does it profit one to allow the desires for these temporary pleasures of the flesh to run rampant, to take hold, and to rule, only for the person to lose his or her beloved soul eternally?" This question is easy to ask. The answers are often difficult. Through God's love and light, we can answer this question. The spiritual clarity comes from God as He directs our spirit homeward toward His Truth. As we allow our spirit to obey, we cleanse our soul and body.

God Gives Free Will

God gives us free will to choose the temporary aphrodisiac or the permanent affirmation—Lo, I am with you in all ways and always through every temptation and arousal of flesh—throughout your life and in the end times. God seeks to renew and restore our spirit every day (2 Corinthians 4:16).

Our Eternal Existence

As I pray and seek God's guidance to counsel and encourage believers and nonbelievers every day, I am more and more convinced that we do not look closely enough into our *eternal existence*. I have found that we are actually mystified by the miracles and handiwork of God. We say, "God is awesome." And rightly so. Because after we know all that we know and all that we can know, we still do not have even one ounce of the knowledge about God's *allness* or what God has planned for the eternal home of those who obey Him. In 1 Corinthians 2:9–10, Paul writes:

> *But as it is written, Eye hath not seen, nor ear heard, neither have entered into the heart of man, the things which God hath prepared for them that love him. But God hath revealed them unto us by his Spirit: for the Spirit searcheth all things, yea, the deep things of God.*

The Psalmist writes, ". . . my heart standeth in awe of thy word" (119:161).

As we fight the uprising of our flesh, God sets an imperative for us to seek Him for His great and accurate knowledge revealed. He (God) longs to fight our battles for us, bless us, and give us peace of mind through the Holy Spirit and His Holy words. This is what saves the soul and makes us know our wholeness in Christ. God never leaves us alone to fight the wiles of the devil or the rulings of flesh. We must seek Him, and not fall victim. This is what saves us and gives eternal life.

What will you give away in exchange for your soul? Will it be a one-night stand? Or a full day of wanton pleasure? Or a lifetime of personal power, material gain, and prestige?

Or, will you seek the power, dominion, and authority of God to be a conqueror of your flesh to help you withstand the egregious workings of unruly flesh and the wiles of the devil? Paul told Timothy that God has not given us the spirit of fear but that of power and of love and a sound mind.

I am convinced that fear is an attempt by the devil to make us "miss the mark" and miss out on God's unfailing favor for our good. Fear seeks to sabotage our soul's quest to abide with Jesus Christ eternally. God promises eternal life. He cannot lie.

How could anyone ever dream of selling a baby, a child, or a spouse? With God's help, I could not. These precious souls are valued more highly than rubies, diamonds, or any material gain. Yet, every day, I counsel men and women who have sold their

God-given souls for the temporary pleasures of this world. They reached for what they thought was the "real thing" and grabbed the quick choice. And they settled for temporary dowry and the sin of a slim season. It is like saying, "Take my soul and give me pleasure for a moment. Who cares about eternal damnation?" This kind of ephemeral "fling" thwarts permanent joy. It blocks the eternal bliss found in a close relatedness with Jesus Christ.

Some church members tell me, "As I line up all my accomplishments, contributions, and earthly deeds, I see myself as a good person." Yet, as they continue to explain their "good works," something still seems to be missing.

This reminds me of the time the biblical David was deeply distressed. He had accomplished great feats for the people of Israel. However, behind a bad decision, the people got very upset with him. They were depressed to the point that their souls were grieved beyond measure. Disappointment had invaded the land, and tougher times didn't seem possible. The real reason their souls were grieved was because they were out of the Will of God. They had to find an outlet for their frustration. David, their hero, became the clear target for releasing their anger, frustration, and displeasure.

He did not try to fix the situation by himself. He knew the source of the real, lasting power—God. The Psalmist goes on to say, "David encouraged himself by having a talk with his God." David talked with God about the men that were upset with him. He told God that his wives and children had been taken from him too. He also knew that unless God would give him strength, he would be in even worse trouble. So, he continued to talk to God until he felt inspired. Then God spoke to David and showed him how he would recover all that had been stolen from them.

It is so imperative that humankind realize the need for the soul's intimate relatedness to God. This frees the soul. No matter what one does to relieve the yearning of the soul, an area of discomfort still lingers that cannot be treated by pain pills, antibiotics, antidepressants, or anti-inflammatory drugs. The truth is, only God can heal the deep hurts, pain, and longing within the soul.

When David was able to have a heart-to-heart conversation with God, he got a distinct answer from Him to go forward, pursue, and conquer. Without this kind of relationship, his soul could have slipped into the same kind of despondency his army had shown. When David restored his close relationship with God, and God gave him the nod to go ahead to pursue and conquer the enemy, He assured David of His sovereignty and providence to recover everything and bless David. This is because with God, nothing that harmonizes the soul with God's Will is ever lost or permanently taken away from us. David was sure of this when he said, "The Lord is my shepherd; I shall not want."

When your soul is grieved with appearances of loss, betrayal, devastation, disappointment, or dejection, consider it a wake-up call to the yearning of your soul. These bellows from deep in the fabric of the soul howl for the restoration of the harmonious relationship of your soul with its eternal Creator and Sustainer. The soul recognizes the God-like spirit as its natural home where God's peace, joy, and unconditional love abide.

Friends, stay aware of God's abiding presence in you. This is essential. It leads you and guides you. It inspires and edifies your soul. It empowers you to fight wisely and courageously in the war on the flesh. Biblical warriors like David, Deborah, and Joshua remembered God's power. They called on it for battle and won. Wear your armor as they did.

Put on your countenance of courage, your helmet of the hope of salvation, and your coat of protection from evil. Cover your heart with the breastplate of righteousness and love. Hold onto your shield of faith. Stand up straight with "your loins girt about with truth" and rightly divide good and evil, using the

Word of God as your staff and spear. Most of all, when you have fought the good fight all you can, continue to stand. Stand firmly on faith in God's unfailing promise of victory over flesh.

SACRED SCRIPTURE

"And in nothing terrified by your adversaries: which is to them an evident token of perdition, but to you of salvation, and that of God."

(Philippians 1:28)

NIV reads:

". . . Without being frightened in anyway by those who oppose you. This is a sign to them that they will be destroyed, but that you will be saved—and that by God."

MEDITATION MOMENT

In Christ I am more than a conqueror. I can do all things as God strengthens me. I am not alone. God, I trust you to lead me and guide me. Feed my spirit with your Spirit. My flesh is under the command of the Holy Spirit. All is well with my soul. Jesus, my Savior and friend, my soul finds complete satisfaction in Your mercy, grace, and love that prevail over all. I realize that You are my Source. My faith is restored. I am strong and ready to do battle with the flesh, for Thou art with me. Amen.

7

✷ LANGUAGES OF THE SOUL PART ONE

The Internet is bringing the continents of the world closer and closer. When I was growing up in the seventies, I thought Asia, Africa, and Europe were a far distance from the United States. Now, as I use the Internet for Bible research, shopping, managing family finances, and communicating for my ministry, I am discovering how close those countries are to my home office or church study.

With a click on my desktop mouse button or a tap on my laptop pad, my local bank is at my fingertips. I can shop in Singapore, San Francisco, or Paris, France, from my den. From my office, I can tap trading centers and services in Africa, Belgium, or South America. I can reach financial centers in Belgium, Italy, or Japan.

The global marketplace, trade centers, and commercial conduits create closeness and convenience for us. They also cause us to think, translate, and talk in different languages—mathematically and verbally. Monolingual is out and bilingual is on its way out. In comes multilingual. It is essential that we speak more than one language to keep up with our shrinking world to compete globally, and to minister to the lost souls wherever they are located.

A Case to Consider

The topic of the importance of language reminds me of a few years ago when my wife Emelda, two sons Mark, Jr. (Marky) and Britton, and I were vacationing in beautiful Puerto Vallarta, Mexico. Among the many planned and unplanned activities of this intended respite was horseback riding. We started out on a mile of flat verdant ground and soon found ourselves leaning forward on our saddles as our horses began to climb dirt and rock inclines. As I looked off the trail to my side, my eyesight was rewarded with a lovely display of fern-green symmetrical mountain ranges. I felt so blessed to see God's handiwork in nature.

Our horses climbed another quarter mile and reached a plateau. They did not stop. By that time, my saddle was beginning to feel warm as it pressed against parts of my body that still had a little feeling. I looked at my wife Emelda and asked, "Are you ready to head back down? I am sore, numb, and tired." She said, "Ditto."

I rode closer to our guide. He was holding the reins of my younger son's horse. I took one glance at Britton to see that he was not a happy camper—not even close. He was looking pale and petrified. I could see that he was fighting back imminent tears. He was ready to end the journey. Right then. Right there. So, I told the guide that we had had enough horseback riding and were ready to return to the ranch. He smiled and nodded. "Good," I said to myself. And, instead of turning the horses around, he rode forward—across the plateau.

A pea-sized tear popped out of Britton's big brown eyes, rolled down his cheek, and landed on the tan saddle. "Oh, no," I said out loud before even thinking. The single tear was followed by a stream of many, wetting his face and saturating his shirt.

The more I tried to make our guide understand our need to go back the more he continued to ride forward. I knew there was something definitely wrong with our lines of communication.

Either I wasn't talking correctly or he didn't understand a word I was saying.

So, after we rode another ten or fifteen feet, a light bulb flashed in my mind. As I beckoned for our older son Mark, Jr., I said, "Marky, you have taken Spanish for six years, let's see if it can pay off. Please tell our guide we feel tired, whipped, beat, and sore. We are aching and in pain, and want to go back to the ranch."

Marky began to make all kinds of excuses about how he had been away from Spanish lessons for a couple of years and had forgotten some of the language. I said with a slight edge in my voice, "Just tell him we want to go back." Simple enough, I thought.

So, Marky finally rode up to the guide and began to speak Spanish. The guide turned to him with a big smile. He was delighted that he could understand Marky's Spanish. Speaking Spanish, he told Marky he would take us back. Just like that.

The trail guide turned the horses around, and we headed back to the ranch. In unison, everyone sighed a chorus of relief. For the next ten minutes, the guide, who basically had been silent for an hour and a half, began to talk 50 miles an hour because he had found someone who knew his language.

I thank God that Mark Jr. was riding with us, and that his Spanish had paid off. Later, Marky told us that we had gone only half the distance of the tour, when he finally made the guide understand our need to turn around and head back to the ranch. Thank God Marky could speak Spanish.

Speaking a New Language

When a person learns to speak a second language fluently, he or she may soon abandon the first-learned language or native language. This might be due to politico-economic or cultural pressure such as was found among the Japanese living in America, American Indians, and those who once spoke Celtic languages in Europe.

Long-term abandonment, infrequent usage, or isolation from the extended usage can lead to the total disappearance of the native language from the person's usage—spoken or written. As it becomes non-existent in the person's life, the person begins to practice the new language in spoken and written form, distinct dialect, and in morals.

Also, new behavior emerges in customs, ethics, etiquette, and mannerisms. It becomes habitual behavior. These are not biologically determined. They have been transmitted culturally from one generation to another.

The Soul's Communication

Throughout our lifetime, we transmit language to our human souls from generation to generation and from hour to hour, day to day, month to month, and year to year. The language comes from our spirit through our thinking. It can be positive or negative.

A pattern of negative language of the spirit makes its imprint on the soul to such an extent that the soul responds likewise and, over time, experiences *dis-ease*. Later, the body acts out this imprint unconsciously, yet visibly. It could show as evil deeds and wicked works.

We must turn a twist on the destruction that we cause to ourselves through unacceptable, outmoded, and extinct language. We must begin by removing the seeds of doubt. We must stop warped reasoning about the Word of God. We must stand firm on His unfailing promise of peace, joy, harmony, and health for the soul.

> *Thou wilt keep him in perfect peace, whose mind is stayed on thee: because he trusteth in thee.*
>
> —Isaiah 26:3

Jesus Speaks Truth

We must learn the language of our Lord and Savior Jesus Christ today and forever. He is our safety and security. He is our refuge and solid rock. He gives the gift of salvation for peace, joy, and eternal life. As we trust in Him, we return our souls to the bliss of primal Eden. Our bodies find their natural home of health, harmony, well-being, and eternal life.

We must relanguage the human spirit to save the soul from negativity, decay, and destruction. The next two chapters show the way. They are designed and written to teach you how to study the new languages of the soul. Study them, learn them, and practice them until you grow fluent in their expressions. This new skill in speaking in God's language will heal, renew, and restore your precious soul.

8

✱ LANGUAGES OF THE SOUL PART TWO

For in him we live, and move, and have our being.

—Acts 17:28

Because of the importance of the saving of your soul, Part Two and Part Three of "Languages of the Soul" are dedicated to you—a wondrous handiwork and beautiful creation of God. Further, these edifying chapters will enable you to relanguage the communication of the human spirit to heal the human soul and restore its life and wholeness.

Let this mind be in you, which was also in Christ Jesus.

—Philippians 2:5

When we relanguage our communication with the soul, we redirect our spirit from evil, error thinking, and unrighteousness. We turn our faith toward God, works of righteousness (right thinking), and repentance (showing godly sorrow and turning away from erroneous ways). We constantly cry out to God to "create a clean heart and renew a right spirit within us."

This becomes the "battle cry" for the Holy Spirit to work in your spirit to redirect your thinking to its like-mindedness. This renews and restores the soul to respond to the perfect Will of God. By letting go of our willfulness, we allow God to walk with us in the newness of life.

Our good word becomes our wand. Our Christlike talk manifests as our new walk. We begin to walk aright (John 14:26; 16:13; Hebrews 8:10). Enter into this new covenant to create a changed lifestyle. This new way of speaking God's Word gives us a sacred language for the reborn soul.

This new way requires practicing the languages of *prayer, worship, praise, meditation, reverence,* and *music.* We must practice these earnestly, joyfully, and respectfully every day to keep the soul renewed and revived.

The Language of Prayer

> *The effectual fervent prayer of the righteous availeth much.*
>
> —James 5:16

Prayer is food and fuel for the soul. When we pray, we speak from "whose we are" and to what Jesus Christ means to us. Just as we call people by their chosen name to get their attention, so do we call our Lord and Savior Jesus Christ by His name.

No matter who we are in rank, title, position, or authority, we all receive the same inclining ear from Jesus when we pray because He taught us to pray, "Our Father . . . ." Neither is Jesus a respecter of persons based on cultural or ethnic differences, social status, or financial conditions. And God hears all, irrespective of native language (English, French, Spanish, Swahili, Ibo).

When you pray, what do you call our God who hears our prayers? Here are some starters:

Jehovah-Jireh: Our provider—(Genesis 22:14)
Jehovah-Ropheka: Our healer—(Exodus 15:26)

Jehovah-Shalom:	The Lord our peace—(Judges 6:23-34)
Jehovah-Shammah:	The Lord is present-there always—(Ezekiel 48:35)
Jehovah-Elyon:	Our Lord most high—(Psalms 7:17)
Jehovah-Roi:	The Lord is my shepherd—(Psalms 23:1)
El Shaddai:	God almighty to supply all the needs of His people—(Genesis 17:1)
Rose of Sharon:	Strength and beauty—(Song of Solomon 2:1)
Lily of the Valleys:	Sweet fragrance—(Song of Solomon 2:1)

Also, in prayer do you call God Prince of Peace or bright morning star? Or Hosanna, Lamb of God, lover of my soul, Father, or Mother? Or just simply call Him Jesus—our All in All?

The language of prayer is spiritual. It heals emotional wounds, physical afflictions, financial woes, heartache, disappointment, grief, stress and strain, and family problems. Prayer is our closest communion with God. It keeps us in an intimate relationship with Him. Learn to pray every day, not only in your desperate extremity. Regular prayer is as natural to our souls as bodily functions like breathing, digestion, and heartbeats.

Also, when you pray, remember to take the limits off God. He is unlimited. Don't try to negotiate with God or tell Him how to "fix" your situation. If you knew how to fix it, you would not need to pray to God. Let go and allow God to do His good and perfect work in your situation.

Pray about your situation in spirit. Talk to God in His language: health, peace, joy, abundance, truth, wisdom, faith, understanding, love, power, goodness, grace, mercy, zeal, life.

Also, speak words of truth about God's nature when you pray, and you will see your prayer life take on a new form of faith. You will find results beyond your most creative imaginings. You will experience excitement beyond verbal description. Pray believing that God doesn't *have* what you want. He *is* what you want as your healer, Good Shepherd, provider, and peacemaker.

★ What is your prayer language?

The Language of Worship [worth-ship]

Worship comes from "worth" (value) and ship (skill or art). It is the skill or art of expressing one's worth or value.

When we know our "worth," we can express "whose we are" as sons and daughters of Jesus in spirit and in truth. Our "worth" is our heritage in God. With God as our Father, we are heirs to His Kingdom of life, love, joy, peace, harmony, happiness, radiant health, and general well-being. Claim your birthright now to experience yourself as the worthwhile and worthy creation of God that you are. Just as God cares for the sparrow and the lilies of the field, He cares for you—His chosen one.

What is God worth to you?

How do you express God's worth?

You can express what God is worth to you through giving of your time, talent, treasure, and tithe to the body of Christ. In so doing, you will multiply your financial increases, and be able to bless the lives of others.

> *Eye hath not seen, nor ear heard, neither have entered into the heart of man, the things that God hath prepared for them that love him.*
>
> —I Corinthians 2:9

★ What is your language of worship?

The Language of Praise

O magnify the Lord with me, and let us exalt his name together.

—Psalms 34:3

Praise is a high level of recognizing and acknowledging the Most High God. It is only when we spontaneously recognize God's presence, power, and activity of blessings in our lives that we genuinely praise God. Praise must come from our experience with the goodness of God—not from some evangelistic "puppeteer" pulling our spiritual strings to make us open our mouths, clap our hands, stomp our feet, or fall prostrate from some emotional hype.

Genuine praise to God comes from the inner source—the heart, soul, and spirit—which recognizes and acknowledges the holiness of God expressed through the Holy Spirit.

The Hebrew word for praise is *hillel*. This is an onomatopoetic semitic root meaning "cry aloud." It is no wonder that our most common word for praise is "Hallelujah!" This is interpreted as "Praise Ye, Jehovah!" (Psalms 113-118; 136; and 145).

The praises that deeply cleanse the soul are not rituals or rights stemming from man-made traditions. They are spontaneous, heartfelt, and genuine responses to God's wondrous power working in and through you, me, and others.

Physical health, financial freedom, saved souls, comfort to the bereaved, and the birth of a healthy baby are just some of the praiseworthy outcomes of ardent prayer and worship language. Other forms of praise such as music, dance, and tongues will be explained later in this chapter.

Whose praise is not of men, but of God.

—Romans 2:29

Through hearty praise, the human spirit invokes the soul to stir the body to magnify God. Praises shall continually cleanse the soul and heal all circumstances in God's divine order.

★ What is your new praise language?

9

✴ LANGUAGES OF THE SOUL PART THREE

So far, I have shown you languages of prayer, worship, and praise. I pray you are growing in your *language for the soul* fluency. Part Three guides you through higher levels of soul communication in languages of meditation, reverence, and music.

The Language of Meditation

Meditation is silent communion focused on God. When we pray, worship, and praise God, we do a lot more talking (except for some forms of sacred worship—worth-ship) than listening. Effective language is two-way. The language of meditation is mostly one-way. We listen as God reveals Himself to us.

We must find a place to get quiet each day. As we do, we must hear God as He talks to us. (My sheep know my voice.) He tells us He's ours and we are His. In meditation we answer Jesus' voice, which says for us to ". . . enter into thy closet, and when thou hast shut the door . . ." (Matthew 6:6). This is when we have shut out all external distractions to hear God's voice.

As you desire God's communication, He will give you what you need in this "listening to God" mode of languaging for the soul.

Some of my best meditations come when I sit in the silence of my home office, lie on the church altar, or lie alert in bed in the wee hours of the morning. These are times when God whispers to me, "I am here." Or "Be still and know." Or simply, "My son, I am with you."

These are the times when I get myself in a full listening mode to hear from God. With no personal preempting, God constantly shows me answers to my congregation's needs and deep concerns.

Also, He has healed my body, comforted my grief, mapped out sermons, and shown ways to further edify the body of Christ. Through meditation, I find peace, joy, inspiration, and a closer understanding of God's purpose and plan in my life.

Getting Yourself Ready to Meditate

If you find your soul in a quandary about your life's purpose or destiny, begin to meditate daily. First of all, be willing and open to listening to God. Believe that God is everywhere present and all-knowing. He knows you inside and out. After all, He created you. He knows your sitting down and uprising, every thought in your head, and every action you anticipate (Psalm 139). You can trust in God's omniscience.

Knowing this truth, you can gain confidence, courage, and strength in meditation. Peace and understanding will follow as you continue consistently. You will harmonize your relationship with God, humankind, and this global society in which we live.

> *Your father knoweth what things ye have need of, before ye ask him.*
>
> —Matthew 6:8

Meditation heals in body, spirit, and soul.

> *Trust in the Lord with all thine heart; and lean not unto thine own understanding.*
>
> —Proverbs 3:5

★ What is your language of meditation?

The Language of Reverence

The language of reverence is an outpouring of love and deep respectful feeling toward God. It is an address of adoration to God. At Pentecost (A.D. 30), in addition to the "mighty wind" and the "tongues parting asunder like as of fire," the disciples spoke "with other tongues, as the Spirit gave them utterance" (Acts 2:4).

Also, according to Peter, the gift of the conversion of Cornelius and his household was the same as what happened at Pentecost (1 Corinthians 10:46; 11:15). The gift of tongues (e.g., speaking in tongues or in a tongue) is a remarkable form of reverence.

In reverence through tongues we feel the presence of the Holy Spirit as an extra surge of spiritual energy, enthusiasm, and excitement. This is an anointing from God which affirms our value as children of our most benevolent Father. Jesus said, "I am the vine; ye are the branches. He that abideth in me, and I in him, the same bringeth forth much fruit; for without me ye can do nothing."

—John 15:5

As the spirit of God wells up within us through our reverence, our spirit becomes subservient in the presence of the Lord. Our own words become inadequate compared to the spontaneous language prompted by the Holy Spirit. As we then surrender our will to God's, we feel the anointing through the outpouring of the gift of tongues. Our organs of speech quicken and produce the stammering of lips and syllabication only possible by the outpouring of the Holy Spirit.

For with stammering lips and another tongue will he speak to this people.

—Isaiah 28:11

As we yield and speak in tongues, the language becomes fluent, flowing, and flowery.

> *Holy men of God spake as they were moved by the Holy Ghost.*
>
> —2 Peter 1:21

Gifts of Reverence

So often when I am down on my knees, giving reverence to God and allowing the outpouring of the Holy Spirit, something comes over me. I find myself jumping to my feet and clapping my hands to praise God. Then the tears begin to stream down my face. The next thing I know, I am speaking in other tongues as the spirit of God gives the utterance.

Now, if the Holy Spirit is not still working in this day and age, somebody should have gotten to me about 37 years ago, because since that day, I have been growing in grace and in the awareness and knowledge of the Holy Spirit. It is alive, well, and working today. Today, the Holy Spirit is real in my soul.

> *And when Paul had laid his hands upon them, the Holy Ghost came on them; and they spake with tongues, and prophesied.*
>
> —Acts 19:6

WHAT ABOUT TONGUES?

Church pastors, theologians, and Bible scholars experienced in exegesis and hermeneutics are divided on their beliefs about the gift of "tongues." I believe the devil does not want the human soul to know the Morse code of the free soul. Reverence through tongues is not an earthly emotional experience. It is a miracle that happened on the day of Pentecost (A.D. 30). It launched a new communicative revolution for the church age—

a vital language of the soul spoken in reverence to God and to edify the soul.

> *He that speaketh in an unknown tongue edifieth himself; but he that prophesieth edifieth the church.*
>
> —1 Corinthians 14:4

Speaking in tongues uplifts the soul. When the soul is down and out and the challenges of this world sit upon the shoulders of men and women, it needs a time of nurturing and edification. This spirited language of tongues that has been granted to the body of Christ will help relieve suffering. Surely, it will lift the human spirit to bring light to the soul.

> *For he that speaketh in an unknown tongue speaketh not unto men, but unto God: for no man understandeth him; howbeit in the spirit he speaketh mysteries.*
>
> —1 Corinthians 14:2

Satan cannot interpret tongues or reverse your blessing from the Holy Spirit. Also, God would not send anything that would bring confusion into the church. When your soul is at stake, you must ensure deliverance and victory for your most precious possession—your eternal soul.

> *For God is not the author of confusion, but of peace, as in all churches of the saints.*
>
> —1 Corinthians 14:33

The language of reverence is an inward-out expression of the wonder-working power of the Holy Spirit. It taps at the door of your soul to remind you of your *true* and living Jesus Christ. Reverence helps you feel your respectful relationship with Jesus Christ.

★ What are your words of reverence?

The Language of Music

> *Sing aloud unto God our strength: make a joyful noise unto the God of Jacob. Take a psalm, and bring hither the timbrel, the pleasant harp with the psaltery. Blow up the trumpet in the new moon . . . .*
>
> —Psalm 81:1–3

The Book of Psalms is packed with prayers, thanksgiving, and praises to God in poetry, hymns, songs, and dance. It is truly the home for the soul because it satisfies devotional needs. It affirms safety and security (secret place of the Most High), closeness with the Infinite, comfort for the grieving, faith for the fearful, and nourishment for the spiritually hungry. The Psalms supply living water for the thirsty and sweetness for the bitter soul. They assure true soul satisfaction.

MUSIC SOOTHES THE SOUL

In addition to the *Book of Psalms,* the rich poetic lyrics of Miriam's song (Exodus 15), the song of Moses (Deuteronomy 32 and 33), and the song of Deborah (Judges 5) provide a profound outpouring of language to inspire the spirit and soothe the soul.

Hannah's song of *Praise* (1 Samuel 2:2–10), Solomon's song of *Love* (Song of Solomon 2:10–15), Mary's song of *Grand Praise* (Luke 1:46–55), and the exaltation of Jesus (Philippians 2:9–11) serve to strengthen the bond of the soul to God's grace.

★ What is your song for the soul?

The Language of Dance

The language of dance comes from the soul's response to the vibrations of music—both in lyrics and instruments. When we dance in the Spirit, our soul prompts our body to respond to the melody of the Holy Spirit and our human spirit. We move our feet, hands, and head in a spiritually rhythmic pattern transmitted from spirit to soul to body. We sometimes shuffle our feet in a spiritual two-step. Other times we leap, run, and skip to the language of music ministering to the soul. This strengthens and fortifies the soul. It frees the soul and causes us to feel joyful.

After David placed the Ark of the Covenant in the "City of David" (after bringing it from the house of Obededom), establishing Jerusalem as the center of worship for the Israelites, he felt victorious. He celebrated his triumph with a corybantic, wild, and ecstatic dance. As he broke into dance "before the Lord with all his might" (2 Samuel 6:12-23), he stripped all of his girded linen (ephod) and danced scarcely covered in frenzied excitement.

He leaped, whirled, and shouted before the Lord (and handmaids of his servants) to the sound of various instruments and highly spirited singing. Truly David danced to the language of the soul—freely and unabashedly. He glorified God.

The language of dance keeps you in step with Jesus' intimate fellowship (for Thou art with me—Psalm 23:4). Dance uplifts and energizes your soul.

★ What new dances will you do to express the "language of dance"?

The Languages of the Soul—Postscript

The languages of the soul call us to be multilingual in spiritual language to build up the body of Christ. God understands

all languages He has given us. He especially calls us to learn and regularly communicate these languages of the soul:
- Prayer
- Worship
- Praise
- Meditation
- Reverence
- Music
- Dance

These keep us focused on God's sovereignty, omniscience, providence, and power. You will truly express your eternal bliss and find lasting peace when you learn and practice the languages of the soul. While the Holy Spirit guides, your fluency will free you in mind, body, and spirit. God will restore your soul.

10

✴ Receiving God's *ISness*

The world-renowned Swiss psychologist Carl Gustav Jung (1875–1961) researched extensively on the nature of the soul. Referring to it as *psyche* (Greek word for soul), he said that humans exhibit a spiritual "thirst" for wholeness.

Writing "that God exists" and that faith was the "core of his patients' issues," Jung devoted considerable counseling time to alcoholics. He learned a lot about their "thirst" and the destructive drinking that never fulfilled their longing.

Jung found alcoholics' "craving for alcohol to be equivalent to a low level of the spiritual thirst for wholeness. In medieval language this was described as the union with God . . . ."[4]

In Latin the term for alcohol is *spiritus*. Alcohol was used for the highest spiritual experience as well as for the most depraved poison."[5] Alcoholics Anonymous (AA) and the *Twelve Steps* programs came out of Jung's work in which he posited that men and women would not "get over" alcoholism until they found God.

During a public lecture given in 1958, one of the founders of AA, Bill W., gave this account:

> *Few people know that the first taproot of AA hit pay dirt some 30 years ago in a physician's office. Dr. Carl Jung, the great pioneer in psychiatry, was talking to an alcoholic patient.*[6]

Through the work of Jung, and God's grace and mercy, this alcoholic patient found God, religion, and spiritual satisfaction. His soul made union with God and was saved. He never again had an obsession to drink.

As a church pastor, I have found a similar pattern in my practice of spiritual counseling. I have seen obsessive behavior cured when lost souls became converted by the infilling of the Holy Spirit. These newly saved souls discovered the power of the living Christ to cure obsessive behavior. Many had been alcoholics, workaholics, drug addicts, sex offenders, prostitutes, overeaters, and sexaholics. I have witnessed their complete healing as they repented, found God, and stayed saved.

Filling Every Thirst

This is likened to the situation of the Samaritan woman whom Jesus met at the well (John 4:1-42). She had come to the well to fill her water pot with water. In this systematic discourse between Jesus and the woman, Jesus talked about "living," flowing water as a sign of eternal life that comes from the true source—God. Also, Jesus helped the woman see that He is the gift of life—giving living water.

When we drink of Him (the Holy Spirit), we will never thirst—not for alcohol, drugs, or false fulfillment through pornography, sex, or harmful food and beverages. Through His revelation of the Holy Spirit, Jesus, the permanent satisfaction for all thirsts, ministered to the Samaritan woman at her moment of critical need.

With the many married men and lovers in her life, she did not know how to quench her thirst for sexual fulfillment. Jesus told her, "Whosoever drinketh of the water that I shall give him ... shall be in him a well of water springing up into everlasting life" (John 4:14).

The woman immediately implored Jesus, "Sir, give me this water, that I thirst not, neither come hither to draw" (John 4:15). She believed the water would quench her thirst and stop her frequent visits to draw water from the well. However, what Jesus tried to help her to see was that His living water (the Holy Spirit) would quench her thirst for sex and the lust of the flesh permanently.

My friend, if you thirst today, take your empty cup (soul depleted by obsession to sin) to the wellspring of Jesus Christ. Ask Him to fill your cup to overflowing with living water (Holy Spirit), so that you may never thirst again. As you drink from God's Word, He will meet you right where we are in need. You will receive His power to save you from sin.

In Psalm 139 we discover the everywhere present, all-knowing, and powerful God. Throughout this chapter the Psalmist reveals God's omnipresence (7–12) and creative power (13–18). This works for us personally and spiritually. This passage confirms God's sovereignty and helps us realize God's *ISness*. He is alpha and omega—the beginning and the end. God knows all, sees all, and *is* all.

God's ISness *Prevails*

When Moses asked God what to tell the Hebrew people about who sent him to them to free them from Pharaoh in Egypt, God told Moses to tell them, "I AM THAT I AM" sent you (Exodus 3:14). God said, "I AM THAT I AM." God is constant—never changing, never ending, and never failing. He is always present as *ISness*. The same I AM created the universe when He imposed order upon chaos and light upon darkness.

God (I AM) created you and me in His I AM likeness, and He does not depart from that which He creates like Himself. He assures us that in His I AM *ISness* He is with us always and in all ways. Thereby, we can confidently confirm: For I am persuaded that neither life nor death, nor power, nor poverty, nor position or title, nor disappointment or rejection, nor anything else in this lifetime shall separate us from the love of God, which is in Christ Jesus our Lord (from Romans 8:38–39).

God's *ISness* is faithful to us (Deuteronomy 7:9). Also, God's faithfulness is *forgiving, holiness* (whole spirit), *just* (Zephaniah 3:5), *merciful* (Psalm 100:5 and 103:17), *patient* (2 Peter 3:9), *truthful* (Deuteronomy 32:4), *kind* (Psalm 54:4), and *loving* (Jeremiah 31:3).

God's *ISness* assures us that He put His Spirit within us and causes us to live in His image and likeness. *ISness* helps us walk according to His commandments (Ezekiel 6:6–7), just as automatically as we breathe.

God beckons us to accept His *ISness*. And we do so by knowing who God is and whose we are as His sons and daughters of the Father. As such, we see ourselves as joint-heirs with Christ. Paul said that great things are prepared for those who know God. As we believe this, hidden treasures, undeveloped talent, untapped ability, and undiscovered genius find their births in our soul. What God has joined together through His spirit cannot be "rent" by beast or man. In the blessed assurance of *ISness* is God's promise: "Beside me there is no God" (Isaiah 44:6). God is.

The Proper Response to ISness

For the person who has taken God for granted; or for that person who has been confused by all the different opinions and teachings about God, ask her or him for wisdom to find things for which to be grateful. Give praise and thanksgiving for simple things like the breath of life and the light of day. Thank God for creating you in His likeness and in His image. Thank Him for teaching you about where the "real you" will spend eternity. Thank the Lord that you did not die in ignorance, in foolishness, in doubt, or in lack of belief in God's *ISness*. Thank God for loving you by redeeming your soul. Thank Him for the gift of salvation.

God said, "I will be your keeper; I will keep you in perfect peace whose mind is stayed on me" (from Isaiah 26:3). You must realize that the soul is not an invalid. Actually, God validates the soul. He said, "I will go with you, to fight for you, to defeat your enemy" (from Deuteronomy 20:4)."

Also, "I AM THAT I AM" will be whatever you need Him to be and whenever. You must not respond to God with a wish box, a hope chest, or a "Santa Claus" mentality. You must respond to God with faith in the Word of God. God's *ISness* will supply all your needs. He is your friend. He is your hope, your battle-ax, and stabilizer. He is your new employment. He is the one who ties up your loose ends. He covers your back. He is your all. As El Shaddai, God Almighty, He is the power to supply all the needs of His people.

The human soul will never be satisfied until it knows the permanent relationship between the Holy Spirit and the human spirit. The soul longs to receive God's *ISness*. It intuitively knows *ISness* as a constant that never changes, never falters, and never fails. The soul seeks *ISness* as *ISness* seeks to satisfy the soul. It is the living water that always flows. Open your spirit to receive God's *ISness*. You will never thirst.

SACRED SCRIPTURE

"God is our refuge and strength, a very present help in trouble. Therefore will not we fear, though the earth be removed, and though the mountains be carried into the midst of the sea.... There is a river, the streams whereof shall make glad the city of God, the holy *place* of the tabernacles of the most High. God is in the midst of her; she shall not be moved: God shall help her, and that right early.... Be still, and know that I am God...."

(Psalm 46:1–10)

MEDITATION MOMENT

Like the woman at the well, today, I come thirsty. Fill my cup, Lord. Fill it with Your Living Water. Fill it till I want no more. Let it overflow to make me whole. I use the wealth of God's living water to share life, love, and vitality as I minister to others. I live and move in God's *ISness*. He is my refuge and peace. My soul resonates with God's *ISness*—flowing as living, loving waters from God to fill my soul. Amen.

11

✸ Your Satisfied Soul

As I counsel parishioners and people outside my church, I continually find the bulk of their problems, concerns, and issues surrounding four areas: personal relationships, family, finances, and health. Where personal relationships are concerned many say, "I can't get along with people at work, at home, and at church."

Some of the families I counsel face break ups, abusive behavior, and teenage suicide. When the troubled children of these families confide in me, I find a deeply-rooted personal unhappiness.

Churched and unchurched families seek relief from the burdens brought by overspending, overdue bills, hound-like creditors, and imminent bankruptcy. As I probe deeper, I find that these individuals, in their pursuits of happiness, live way beyond their means to appear successful and "keep up with the Joneses."

The ones who discuss their problems with sickness describe the frustrations from arthritis, diabetes, high blood pressure, kidney failure, and heart disease.

As these unsatisfied souls describe their quest for happiness, I see them walking through a self-made lifestyle maze. They go in and out and round about towards something they think will solve all their life's ills.

Soul Robbers

To find joy, many say they take expensive exotic trips. When they vacation, they go on adventurous outdoor sports extravaganzas or spend time at resorts on "paradise" islands with a spouse or significant other. Others buy expensive jewelry, perfume, and sports cars.

Then, there are those who seek lovers and multiple sex partners for comfort and company. Others shower friends or family with lavish gifts. Often, people tell me how they spend their money on the best brand-name fashions for self-satisfaction, praise, and validation. They seek to be seen with the well-known, rich, and in-crowd to feel powerful and highly esteemed.

Many live beyond their financial means to " be somebody" to themselves, their families, friends, church members, and coworkers. I am amazed to find that still others go so far as to strive to impress their enemies.

Still others get educated and trained for six-figure salaries. A few rationalize that they are trying to impress God—all for personal "happiness." They seek "joy" from external sources. These artificial pacifiers do not reward the soul with joy and permanent peace.

Those who were persistent enough to reach the end of the materialistic matrix found that just as they stepped into the happiness square, they found their happiness to be short-term, unrealistic, or merely ephemeral—there and then gone. Soon they desired a deeper and longer ecstasy.

In this descriptive discourse about the unsatisfied soul, I have been addressing a real problem in the end times. The constant outward movement toward happiness in the outer realm causes these "happiness-seekers" to move away from the internal realm of their true soul satisfaction.

Supplying the Soul

The inward direction draws us toward the kind of joy that reaches the seat of the soul. It is lasting, true, tangible, valid, and wholesome. The inward nurtures and heals the soul. It feeds, nourishes, and soothes the soul to secure peace for our very heart, mind, and body. Our souls long for the inward direction toward Jesus Christ and are satisfied only when we steer our minds, hearts, attitudes, and actions toward that homeward path.

Different from the tortuous materialistic maze, the soul's inward path to Christ is straightforward, forthright, and direct. It guides us, instructs us, warns, and corrects us. It coaches and counsels us along the way. It guides us to safety and security. It guarantees true and lasting joy, health, and wholeness. It perpetuates spiritual prosperity and peace of mind. It is lasting.

Friends, now is the time to turn a twist on the outward direction to happiness. Take the inward path. This movement leads to a satisfied soul.

The inward direction toward soul satisfaction reminds me of the Israelites as they were following the guidance of God to escape Pharaoh in Egypt. They did not finally get rid of Pharaoh until they had crossed the water. This long narrow sea that lies between Asia and Africa is called the Red Sea. The Israelites—with the Egyptians of Pharaoh's court on their heels—crossed it as God changed it to dry land. When the water returned, Pharaoh's Egyptians (chasing after the Israelites to bring them back into bondage) drowned.

To reach our blessed home of joy and peace—the satisfied soul—we must cross a Red Sea. As God parts the waters, He guides us to rightly divide His words of truth, love, and life to create right thinking and right actions. Crossing over the dry land represents a spiritual process from which our actions toward the erroneous outward approach to happiness and fulfillment are brought into subjection to conform to God's standards. This keeps us on the homeward path to true soul satisfaction.

The steps of the journey inward include

- Faith in God to obey His Will
- Repentance (godly sorrow for sins and transgression)
- Turning to God for forgiveness for our sins
- Baptism of the Holy Spirit—the whole spirit of God that saves us and gives life
- Holy living, according to the Word of God (Hebrews 12:14).

Following through on these brings healing to the soul. These give new life to the body and spirit.

You can stay on the inner path to soulful living through speaking the languages of the soul. Also, walk with God and with all His people to stay under-girded with spirited activities that keep your soul satisfied. Just some of these include

- Daily devotions
- Bible reading
- Bible classes/seminars
- Daily prayer
- An enjoyable hobby or business
- Meditation
- Sports and physical fitness

Also practice

- Sharing the good news with others
- Keeping a daily journal about your spiritual journey
- Keeping a positive sense of humor
- Showing gratitude

- Exercising in the outdoors (walking, biking, golfing, swimming, hiking, and gardening)
- Keeping a prayer partner who is on the inner path

These feed the soul and help to keep our attention focused on optimism, praise, thanksgiving, and the goodness of God. We learn to appreciate the handiwork of God's creation. We reaffirm God's *ISness*. We keep a close relationship with God.

Regular spiritual practices renew and restore our faith. They help us know and acknowledge God's omniscience, omnipotence and omnipresence working in our lives and the universe. They help us build fluency in speaking languages of the soul.

Today, people who continue to turn to the Holy Spirit for genuine soul satisfaction report true and lasting rewards. Let's take a look at some they have shared with me:

- Peace of mind
- Complete healing from drugs and substance abuse, obesity, high blood pressure, cancer, and heart disease
- Deliverance from arrogance, know-it-allness, false pride, haughtiness, and selfishness
- Recovery from workaholism to find real meaning and joy in life
- Using creative talent and spiritual gifts to volunteer in church auxiliaries (stewardship, discipleship, music ministry, prayer, children and youth ministry, prison ministry, Bible teaching, church leadership and management, prayer team ministry, hospital and sick and shut-in ministries).
- Giving tithe, talent, time, and treasure generously within the church. (You can't beat God giving.)

The spirit stays uplifted by the Holy Spirit. The satisfied soul stays anchored in Truth.

SACRED SCRIPTURE

"For he satisfieth the longing soul, and filleth the hungry soul with goodness."

(Psalm 107:9)

MEDITATION MOMENT

God, you are my Source. As I abide in You continuously, You walk with me and talk with me night and day. You stay with me along the straight path to the true satisfaction of my soul. You instruct me and reassure me. I feel encouraged, inspired, and comforted. I find new hope for today and tomorrow. My attention is turned inward to Your goodness. Thank you, God, for satisfying my soul. Amen.

12

✷ Caring for the Soul

When I was a little boy, I could often tell when my mother was experiencing an unusually challenging day. As she went about her household duties, she would hum the old spiritual, "Christ Is All." Some of its lyrics are

> Christ is all. He's everything to me. Christ is all. He rules the land and sea. Christ is all. Without him nothing could be. Christ is all. He's all and all this world to me.
>
> —Kenneth Morris, 1916

The more she hummed the better she felt and the broader she smiled. After a while, I was humming right along with her. And before too long, I was smiling and singing the lyrics. Soon we created a duet of humming and joyful singing.

While singing, we joined hands and moved together with the music. I could feel a stirring in my soul. I felt happy, safe, and secure. Then, something else happened. Her whole countenance transformed from worried to peaceful. That was a powerful experience—two souls, male and female, changed by song.

The soul is nourished through languages of music and dance, when we communicate them lovingly and authentically. As the soul is properly fed and nurtured, *dis-ease* changes to ease. Chaos changes to calmness. Darkness dissipates. The light of God dispels the darkness, bringing order to heal the soul. The soul, in turn, heals the body. This is soulful.

My friend, I urge you to make it a daily practice to stay focused on feeding your soul the finest spiritual nourishment. Nurture your soul as you allow the Holy Spirit to work through your spirit to cleanse and heal. Take time each day for spiritual devotion, prayer, praise, worship, and meditation. Allow yourself to feel God's presence as He speaks to your spirit.

Jesus said that we will surely face personal trials, tests, and tribulations in this lifetime. They help us mature spiritually to know God personally and at a deep spiritual level. Yet, He has given us something greater than these vicissitudes. When we see these works of the devil, vexations, and tough times as soul-makers rather than soul-breakers, we keep our inlook and outlook Godward. This inward direction leads us to victory, and as we stay planted firmly in the Holy Spirit, we bear the fruit of the Spirit:

- Love
- Joy
- Peace
- Patience
- Kindness
- Gentleness

When we talk Spirit-talk, we walk the Spirit-walk.

Powerful Scriptures follow. Use them to continue to care for your soul through these troubled and often vexing end times. Friend, use them to face the problems in your life. Through faith, love, and gentleness, use them to the point of deliverance.

CARE FOR THE *HURTING* SOUL

I prayerfully selected these Scriptures to help you care for the soul as you move through personal tests, trials, and tribulation. Apply them to your specific situation to attain victory in Jesus Christ.

- Doubting Your Faith in God: Psalm 8; Proverbs 30:5; Hebrews 11; 1 John 5:13-20
- Discouraged: Psalm 34; Romans 15:13; Hebrews 6:9-12
- Lonely: Psalm 22, 42; John 14:15-31
- Tempted by Lust or Sex: 2 Samuel 11:1-12:25; 1 Corinthians 6:12-20
- Tired or Feeling Worn Out: James 1:2-6
- Sin Sick: John 3:1-21; Ephesians 1:13-14
- Facing a Difficult Decision: 1 Kings 3; Psalm 139; Colossians 3:12-17
- Afraid: Psalm 27, 91; 1 John 4:13-18
- Thinking about Suicide: Romans 8:35-39

CARE FOR THE *JOURNEYING* SOUL

These scriptures give tender, loving care to tried and tested souls:

- Care Taker: Ephesians 3:14-21
- Sick/Ill: Psalm 23; James 5:14-16
- Facing Empty Nest or Life Alone: 1 Corinthians 7:25-38; 12:1-31
- Widowed: 1 Timothy 5:3-16; 1 John 5:1-5
- Facing Divorce: Psalm 25; Matthew 19:1-9; Philippians 3:1-11
- Bereaved: Romans 8:31-39; 14:7-9; 1 Thessalonians 4:13-18
- Retiring from Work or a Business: Numbers 6: 24-26; Psalm 145; Philippians 4:10-13
- "Broke" or Low Funds: Job 1:13-22; Romans 8:18-39
- Facing Bankruptcy: Ecclesiastes 5:10-20
- Unemployed: Jeremiah 29:10-14
- In Prison: Acts 12:1-9; Psalm 46:10-11

Care for the *Recovering* Soul

Discover the healing power of Jesus Christ through these Scriptures:

- Overcoming Addiction: Proverbs 23:29–35; Ephesians 4:22–24
- Workaholism: Genesis 2:1–3
- Alcoholism: Psalm 40:1–5

Begin to read and apply these Scriptures today. They will give you complete soul satisfaction. You will emerge victorious, giving God the glory.

SACRED SCRIPTURE

"So is my word that goes out from my mouth: It will not return to me empty, but will accomplish what I desire and achieve the purpose for which I sent it."

(Isaiah 55:11 NIV)

MEDITATION MOMENT

Thank you God for creating my soul out of your Spirit by speaking the Word of God. I follow your example by speaking the languages of the Holy Spirit. I put them into my Spirit. They work to heal my soul. My spirit and soul harmonize with my body to form a glorious whole being that enters into your heavenly realm of eternal life.

I am made every whit whole. As the shepherd cares for his sheep, thank You for caring for my soul. Thank you for new life and peace I find in Your tender mercy and unending grace and love. Amen.

13

✳ THE SOULS OF TWO MEN

Often, the relationship between a father and son can be hard to read. Fathers find irony, paradox, and dichotomy as they assume the diverse roles of father, brother, mentor, and friend to their sons. A father must prepare his son for the good and bad times he will face in the future, while admonishing and loving him in the present. I have experienced all these and, I must admit, it's a tough job.

Father and son relationships remind me of God, the Father, and His only begotten Son Jesus Christ. He had to send His only son to suffer scourging by man and to die a vile death. This was to redeem humankind from the original sin of Adam and Eve and to set us free. He gave His Son's life for all—including you and me—to have a right to the tree of life. As a father, I would find that to be a tough job, if not even impossible.

God gave life (His son Jesus) in the *present* for humankind to have eternal life in the *future*. As tough as it was for the Father and the Son, He did it lovingly and distinctly for us.

During my eight years of seeking God in the revelation of the soul, I prayed and fasted. I kept an exceptionally keen ear open to God as He revealed the content for this book. God challenged me, coached, and counseled me. He molded my spirit and mentored me to write this revealed knowledge of the soul. Now, I share this from an even closer standpoint than I ever thought possible.

Many times, while I was writing, I felt as if I was being tested, tried, and sanctified as God prepared me to discern from Him the Truth about the soul. I grew and matured spiritually. I learned to trust God more and more. Now, I can see that this was a period of making me and molding me to conform to God's Will.

Although it was not always easy to deal with the ups and downs, disappointments, frustrations, and uncertainty during what often seemed like a probation period, I never doubted God's abiding presence. At times, I seemingly had no concept at all about the soul. Then there were the times when it seemed as if all I learned needed to be scrapped and started over. Other days, God would lead me through Scriptural searches as I pondered this great mystery.

God's way is always perfect, and now I know why this spiritual preparation period was so important (besides the point that God sees all and knows all). Stay with me as I explain.

God blessed my wife Emelda and me with two sons, Mark Curtis Tolbert, Jr. (Marky) and Britton Elliott Tolbert (Britt). Both so different. Both so precious. I want to focus on Mark, Jr. and how his example relates to the human soul.

The Magic of Marky

Marky was quiet at home and loud when he was away from home. A stark difference. However, he was loud in a manner that brought his peers to love him, respect him, and even slightly envy him. This was because even in his bold outer behavior, he never offended anyone. He always showed respect and kept a Christ-like regard for others.

Although loud in behavior, he was never "loud" in his attire. Everything had to match and follow the vogue. For example, from the age of three or four, Marky was not going to leave the house with his clothing wrinkled or not matching. Eventually, his expectation for perfect fashion and form applied to all under the roof of my house. This was for our house and the church members at Christ Temple Church. With endearment, our family named him "the fashion police."

Often, as I was leaving for Sunday morning services, he would chide, "Dad, you're not leaving with *that* tie on, are you?" When I would give him that unquestionable "fatherly" look that said "be quiet and mind your own clothes," he made no hesitation to get his mother involved by yelling, "Mama, please and come see what Daddy has on. Please don't let him out of the house looking like this."

With those frequent "dress downs," he finally trained me to properly mix and match my full attire to go fashionably into the pulpit and on television to do God's work. It's still vivid to me how I would pick a shirt and four or five ties, and then march by Britt and Emelda before my final fashion inspection by Marky. Just because I passed by did not mean that I had passed. Often, Marky would say, "Wait. I've got just the perfect tie to make that look cool." Sometimes it would be the one he had "borrowed" from my tie rack several months before.

I cherish every minute I spent with Marky, my namesake, protagonist, protégé, and friend. How could I have known I was going to have only 19 short-lived years with his positive humor, his beautiful warm smile, and his camaraderie in my life?

Death is so permanent on this earthly side. However, when Martha told Jesus she knew she would see her brother Lazarus again in the great resurrection, Jesus said, "I am the resurrection, and the life: he that believeth in me, though he were dead, yet shall he live" (John 11:25).

While Marky was alive, I so strongly felt his call to ministry. It was a different calling and not necessarily to "pastor." Marky, in his special way, loved people. He was a real people person, and his first love was children. It was an innocent, genuine "love" which I never fully understood.

He was drawn to all children, and they were drawn to him—infants, toddlers, and the "terrible twos." Even as a toddler himself, he would reach for another one, and, before we knew it, Marky was holding him on his lap. Little Titus was one example of this. And even though Titus was about the same size, Marky held him lovingly and securely on his lap as though he were his big brother.

When we brought his baby brother Britton home from the hospital, Marky quickly reached for him. As Britton grew bigger, Marky loved to hold and "father" him. They grew to be typical brothers, and even though they chided each other, Marky wanted to take Britt out with him and his friends on graduation night.

Since he didn't have a younger sister, he "adopted" little Morgan as his sister. Later, he "adopted" Jazzmine (another infant in our church) as his "daughter." I am still trying to figure out how he coined the term "daughter" for little Jazzmine, the daughter of Chris and Le´Rhonda Collier.

As a "kid," Marky never complained. He trusted his parents and grandparents to know what was best for him. He didn't *like* everything we asked him to do, but still he would do it. For example, before going out with his friends on a Friday night, I would remind him that he had forgotten to take out the trash and mop the kitchen floor. He wasn't happy about those household chores, but he would do them, and very neatly. He was always neat and tidy. After finishing, he would tell Emelda and me he was finished and where he was about to go.

When I would ask him if he had enough money, he would say, "Well, I've got 20 dollars." I would pull 40 dollars out of my pocket. As I was handing it to him, he would look at me and say, "Oh, Dad, that's too much. I'll take just 20 dollars more. That should get me through." As his father, I could never believe he would turn down money, but I guess, in his own way, he knew if he really needed money or anything else, his earthly father was willing to supply his needs.

As his father, I never really knew or appreciated the greatness that I had in Marky until he had departed this earth plane. I would never compare Marky to Jesus, but I do believe, by his sterling example, Marky was born into the world to make a difference. Jesus didn't stay among the living long, and neither did Marky. To fully describe how many were blessed by Marky, the testimonials would fill volumes. However, overall, I believe Marky's mission was to point the living to the life of Jesus Christ to the extent that we would draw closer to Him. With Marky's passing, I better understand God's full revelation about the soul. As grievous as I have found his passing, my own soul's journey throughout helped to give this book deeper meaning, firmer continuity, and solid completion.

For example, as I talked to Dr. Martis Jones when she was helping me organize and edit this book, I told her about Robert Mitchell, a friend of mine who has a prophetic ministry gift. Prophet Mitchell did not know that I had been working on *Naked Soul* for some six years, yet he told me about a book I was writing. Although a little stunned at first, I was pleased that God knew enough about this book to let a prophetic word come forth. It confirmed that I was on the right track with His book and my trust in God.

Then Prophet Mitchell said something even more profound. He told me I had another chapter to write. How could he? I thought deeply about the long, laborious years I had searched and researched, listened to God, and uttered daily prayers. I believed God had already given me everything I could write about the soul for this book. Plus, He had given me the divine revelation to enhance the discernment and understanding needed to minister to others. What more could I possibly write about? What more could I ask God to reveal?

A More Recent Revelation

Maybe there was more to write because I had taken care of my wife Emelda during her year and a half battle with breast cancer. With God's love and healing power as the Great Physician, she was cured. Through her arduous healing process, I learned even more about the soul. Most of all, I grew to better understand the woman's soul that trusts God.

Almost one year later, on December 22, 2000, my natural family, church family, friends around the world, and I faced the sudden death of Marky. While driving to his job (he was home on college break), a Kansas City fire truck slammed into Marky's car as it raced to another accident nearby. Marky died within minutes.

The Soul Lives On

After Marky's death in the physical body, it took almost six months for me to see it as a "homegoing" and not a "home leaving." We were so close, and all I could think about was how I could no longer hug him, see him flash his heart-warming smile, smell his many fragrant colognes, hear him complete my sentences, or hear him call me "Daddy." No longer would he finish inspecting me as I was leaving for Sunday morning services. No longer would he play keyboard for my 7:30 a.m. Sunday service. I missed our frequent daily e-mails, phone chats, and instant messages from *America Online*.

I would eat an orange and seem to be eating it for Marky and me. Oranges were his favorite fruit. My golf swing was for Marky and me. We were two entwined as one in heart, spirit, and soul:

my son, "soul tie," namesake, and business partner. It was hard for me to release thoughts about his physical absence.

Although he was gone, I felt his presence at every waking and turning. When I didn't, I longed for it. He was gone and yet still here. Here and yet gone. My soul longed for Marky's presence and humor. Instead, it found grief.

While praying and crying out to God, He showed me the "homegoing" of Marky and how his soul lived on. It was God's divine predestined plan, laid out before he was formed in his mother's womb and before the foundation of the world.

Completing the Journey

Again, those prophetic words rang in my ears. Without even knowing the prophetic utterances from Prophet Mitchell about completing this book, Dr. Martis Jones said, "Bishop, you have one more chapter to write." She stated this with conviction and firmness as she sat across the kitchen table in my family's home. Wow. I knew God was ready to do more soul work in me about the location of the soul, to finish this book and to minister more completely to the world.

This confirmed the prophecy, and I returned to my laptop to finish writing this book. My first thoughts were on the relationship of eternity to the soul. I had written about it and described it in eulogies, and now Marky had experienced it first hand.

Souls Connecting

My comfort lies in knowing that my soul will recognize Marky's soul in heaven. Also, without a shadow of doubt, he will recognize my soul. Then I will again enjoy his soft laughter, warm smile, winning personality, quick wit, care and compassion, and genuine love. Together, we will be able to walk, talk, commune, and glorify God throughout eternity. This assurance is what keeps my soul satisfied until we meet again.

Just knowing I will recognize Marky helps me find peace and comfort. Many church people, fellow pastors, family members, and friends continue to tell me they have dreamed about Marky since his homegoing. They have felt his presence in their dreams. They feel assured of his ongoing soul's journey. Marky's presence has assured them that he is in a better place. He is in the place that we all long to be, for to be absent from the body is to be present with the Lord. That's our permanent *home*.

Bringing Closure

So, as I close this book, I dedicate this last chapter to my namesake. Also, I admonish you to treat your loved ones, church members, coworkers, and customers in a Christ-like manner. Care for them and show concern for them as if it is your last time to be in contact with them.

When Marky told me he would be back after work, I expected him back. After all, he always kept his promises. Also, he was young and on fire for God. You never know when that last time will come.

On the morning of December 22, 2000, Marky took his mother's car to Tom's Auto Shop to get two new tires. I drove Marky's car to the church office. After getting her new tires mounted, Marky drove his mother's car back to my office and gave me her keys. After discovering that I got his key stuck in his ignition, he went to his car and got the key out. He did not hesitate to show me it could be done, as he flashed the key through my office door. I was about ready to go into a meeting. All I could think was, "That's my Marky."

However, I never thought for one minute, especially three days before Christmas, that moment would be the last time I would see my son alive. Two hours later I got a call to come to the hospital. Marky had been in a car wreck. I prayed all the way to the hospital. When I arrived, the hospital chaplain met me, and her sad eyes gave it all away. I knew she was not going to give me any good news.

Five minutes later, the doctors explained how they had tried everything. Broken emotionally and spiritually, I collapsed on the floor. As my brother, Wendell, helped me up, I said I had to go to my son, because if God wanted to show us a miracle, I needed to pray at Marky's bedside. Now. The doctors begged me to wait until they could clean him up and remove the tubes and other life-saving apparatus. But I insisted on going to him right then.

Deacon Bennie Walsh (from our church) and I went into the hospital emergency room and prayed. We called for corporate prayers from church Elders, the church prayer team, and a myriad of other prayer warriors. But Marky did not respond to the ardent appeals of this life. His soul had already departed.

In a state of shock, denial, and disbelief, I could not accept that Marky would not see his goals and plans for the future attained. How could God take him now? How?

The Bible says we are once to be born and once to die. No person knows the day or the hour when God will come for his or her soul, but each one has a predestined time.

Preparing to Live with Loved Ones Forever

Friends, if your loved one has made a homegoing, I urge you to prepare your soul to live with him or her again. You will recognize his or her soul because the eternal soul that is locked inside the earthly body looks just like him or her. Also, locked up inside your body is the "real you." And God holds the key to release your soul for it to live on and on eternally.

As for our two souls—Marky's and mine—we will embrace, rejoice, sing, dance, and give a victory shout when we meet again on God's celestial shores.

O death, where is thy sting? O grave, where is thy victory?

—1 Corinthians 15:55

CHAPTER NOTES

Except where otherwise indicated (e.g., New International Version—NIV), all Scripture quotations in *Naked Soul* are from the King James Version (KJV) of the *Bible*.

Chapter 4: The Scene and Unseen

1. Henry H. Halley. *Halley's Bible Handbook* (Grand Rapids, MI: Zondervan Publishing House, 1965), p. 129.

2. A complete description of the directions and dimensions of the tabernacle are presented in Henry H. Halley. *Halley's Bible Handbook*, pp. 128–133.

3. Ibid., p. 129.

Chapter 10: Receiving God's ISness

4. Stephen Segaller and Merrill Berger. *The Wisdom of the Dream.* p. 181.

5. Ibid.

6. Anthony Star. *The Essential Jung.* pp. 308, 309. Also, refer to Carl G. Jung's *Memories, Dreams, and Reflections* (New York: Random House, 1963).

Chapter 12: Caring for the Soul

This song, "Christ Is All," was written by Kenneth Morris in 1916. The full lyrics and music can be found in church hymnals including *Songs of Zion* (Nashville, TN: Parthenon Press, 1981), p. 180.

INDEX

Acacia 29
Acts 63, 71, 72, 91
Adam v, 1-6, 7, 9-10
Adamah 1, 4
Ahasuerus 8
Alcoholism 51, 77-78, 92
Alcoholics Anonymous 77-78
Altar of Burnt Offering 29
Altar of Incense 31
Ark of the Covenant 32, 75
Arthritis 38, 83
Authority 11, 12, 18, 40, 52, 64

Babylonian Calendar 23
Baptism of the Holy Spirit 20, 86
Beggar 41
Bill W. 77
Body Temple 34, 38
Breast Cancer 100
Britton iii, 58, 96, 98

Candlestick 31
Cherubim 30-32
Christ Temple Church iii, 97
Christmas 23, 103
Collier,
  Chris 98
  Jazzmine 98
  Le'Rhonda iii, 98

Dance 74-76, 89, 104
David 8, 53, 75
Day of Atonement 24, 27, 32
Deborah 54, 74
Dedication 24
Delilah 15
Dis-ease 12, 60, 89
Dominion 11-12, 16, 18, 32, 40, 52

Emelda iii, 58, 96-98, 100
Eve 2-6, 7, 9, 11-12, 17, 47, 49, 95
Esau 7

Fashion Police 97
Feast of Ingathering 27
Feast of the Tabernacle 24, 25, 27
Flesh 2, 4, 12-18, 37, 40-43, 49-51, 53-55
Garden of Eden 3, 5, 16-17, 61

Genesis 5, 7; 9, 64, 65, 92
Great Physician 100

Hebrews 9, 27, 28, 42, 64, 86, 90, 91
Holy of Holies 30-32
Holy Place 30-31

Illinois, Chicago 21, 85
Internet 57
Iowa, Clinton 21, 36, 45
Isaiah 9, 61, 71, 80, 81, 93
ISness 77-82

Jehovah 64-65, 67
Jones, Dr. Martis iii, 99, 101
Joshua 54
Journeying 91
Jung, C. G. 77-78

Kansas City 100

Lamb 25, 65
Lamentations 8, 9
Laver 29
Lazarus 41, 97
Leviticus 25, 27
Living Waters 74
Lust 8, 47-50

Mark, Jr. (Marky) i, v–vi, 15, 58–59, 96–104
Meditation 9, 18, 34, 41, 44, 56, 64, 69–76, 82, 86, 88, 90, 93
Mercy Seat 32
Mexico, Puerto Vallarta 58
Morris, Kenneth 89
Moses 27, 28, 36, 74, 79
Most Holy Place 30–32

Outer Court 28

Paradise 2–6, 7–8
Passover 24–25
Patton, George Smith 38
Paul 13, 46, 51–52, 72, 80
Pentecost 24–25
Pharaoh 27, 79
Philippians 56, 63, 74, 91
Pot of Manna 32
Prayer 8–9, 15–16, 28, 35–37, 49–50, 64–67, 69–76, 86–87, 90
Purim 24

Recovering 92
Red Sea 85
Relanguage 61, 63
Reverence 64, 69, 71–76
Roper, John iii

Samaritan Woman 78
Samson 8, 15
Serpent 5, 11, 16, 47, 49
Shekinah Glory 24
Sheol-Hades 41–42
Spiritus 77
Stewardship 87
Strongholds 14
Substance Abuse 51, 87

Tabernacle 27–32, 37–39, 82
Table of Shewbread 30–31
Tent 27–30, 37
Ten Commandments 12, 13, 27, 28, 32, 47, 80
Theologians 72
Titus 98
Tolbert,
   Aaron iii
   Britton Elliott iii, 58, 96, 98, 111

Carol iii
Emelda iii, 58, 96–98, 100, 111
Lorene iii
Lee, Jr. iii
Lee A., Sr. iii, 111
Mark, Jr. i, v–vi, 15, 58–59, 96–104, 111
Vivian iii
Wendell iii, 103
Tongues 67, 71–73
Tree of Knowledge 7
Twelve Steps Programs 77

Vashti 8

Walsh, Bennie 103
Whit 40, 93
Word of God 8, 9, 13, 16, 39–43, 55, 60, 81, 86, 93
Workaholism 51, 78, 87, 92
Worship 9, 23, 28, 31, 37, 64, 66, 67, 69, 75–76, 90
Worth-ship 66, 69

Yard 28
Yoke 43, 44
Yom Kippur 24

❏ Please mail me additional copies of *Naked Soul*. (book price: $11.95—includes tax and shipping/handling charges).

To place orders, call 816.561.3619 or mail your order using this form. Orders may be faxed to 816.561.1218.

Name _____

Title _____

Organization _____

Address _____

City _____ State _____ Zip Code _____

Phone _____ Fax _____

ACT NOW! Please send me _____ books ($11.95 per book)

Mail to:　　　　　　Christ Temple Church
　　　　　　　　　　3400 Paseo Boulevard
　　　　　　　　　　Kansas City, MO 64109
　　　　　　　　　　U.S.A.

❏ Check ($11.95 per book, payable to Victorious Living Publishing Co.)

Total enclosed $ _____

❏ MasterCard　　　　　❏ VISA　　　　　❏ American Express

Account # _____ Exp. Date _____

Name as it appears on card _____

Signature _____

Contact Mark C. Tolbert to speak at your next church conference, convention, or retreat at:

>Christ Temple Church
>3400 Paseo Boulevard
>Kansas City, Missouri 64109
>(816) 561-3619 (Church)
>(816) 561-1218 (Fax)
>www.bishopmarktolbert.com

ABOUT THE AUTHOR

MARK C. TOLBERT is the senior pastor of Christ Temple Church in Kansas City, Missouri. With over twenty years' experience in soul-stirring expository preaching, teaching, and evangelizing, he makes plain and accessible the meaning of the soul. The world over, Mark Tolbert is identified with sound exegesis, and is bold in his stand for the infallible Word of God. There can be no doubt that he is a living example of the tested soul "on fire" for Jesus Christ.

Known in his community and nationwide for exemplary church leadership, neighborhood and community development, ministries for women, and Christian education, he leads in many elected positions to improve human lives. He led the team that recently built and opened the 2.8 million-dollar Lee A. Tolbert Charter School and the Lee A. Tolbert Recreational Center in Kansas City, Missouri.

Through his global television ministry (Word Network and PAX) and local radio programming, he communicates a positive challenge to more than 17 million viewers. His more than 2,000 church members reflect cultural, ethnic, and social diversity.

He is the husband of 23 years to Emelda Façiane Tolbert and father of two sons, Mark C. Tolbert, Jr. (gone to Glory) and Britton Elliott Tolbert.

Mark Tolbert received his DD from Western Baptist Bible College. His mission is to foster spiritual growth and maturity in the lives of all humanity to enable them to live victoriously and abundantly through the revelatory Word of God.